Suffering in Silence

TURNING PAIN INTO PURPOSE

Darlene Wilkerson Parrish

ISBN 978-1-68526-480-2 (Paperback)
ISBN 978-1-68526-481-9 (Digital)

Covenant Books, Inc.
11661 Hwy 707
Murrells Inlet, SC 29576
www.covenantbooks.com

To my late mother, Juanita S. Wilkerson, who said to me before she passed away, "I wish I could have been more like you," meaning that she wished she had found her voice.

My response was, "No, I wished I could have been more like you, showing love unconditionally."

The word *No* was not in her vocabulary. She gave her all unselfishly. Even if she did not have it, she found a way to get it.

CONTENTS

INTRODUCTION

One reason that I have decided to write this book is because, as a child, I had a lot to say but did not have the courage to say it. I had a story but did not have a voice. Many women, in particular, have experienced unspoken things in their lives in which they are hiding behind a veil. I was one of those women. Like many women, we have a smile plastered on our faces. We suppress our feelings only for them to resurface in other areas of our lives. If you were to remove the veil, you would find the real woman. The woman who has been bruised, broken, and battered. The woman who thinks that she does not matter. The woman who thinks that she is less than. The woman who allows others to take advantage of her. The list goes on.

My desire for you by reading this book is that if you have experienced any of the traumas that I had experienced, you will know there is hope in turning your pain into purpose. You do not have to suffer in silence any longer. You are *somebody*. You *matter*. You are *worthy*. You have a *voice*. All you have to do is start talking. Someone out there will listen. Create your own platform to be heard. That is how my book was birthed. Instead of waiting for a platform to share my story, my truth, I created my own platform. What is your story? What is your truth?

I grew up in a rural area in North Carolina. My family consisted of my mom, dad, four brothers, and one sister. We had what appeared to be a happy and normal family. My dad always worked two jobs. He worked with the state and owned a tobacco farm. He was the disciplinarian. My mother worked with the state also. She was the nurturer, the spoiler. She made sure that we always had what we needed and wanted. She was a giver. She gave from her heart. She gave her last literally. If she had a light bill due and someone had a light bill due as well, she would give her light bill money to them if their bill was due first and the person needed it. If she had, the neighbors also had. You can best believe that no one was ever hungry in her presence. She fed the multitude. "No" was not in her vocabulary. She helped others in every way imaginable. She had a servant's heart. As I grew into adulthood, I saw a great deal of traits that we shared.

Growing up, I did not think we were rich, but I thought that we had some money simply because we were one of the first ones in the neighborhood to get a house phone. We were one of the first ones to get carpet in our home. We were one of the first ones to get running water in our home. Well, we already had running water. We had to run to the spring and get the water. To rephrase that, we were one of the first ones to get indoor plumbing—a sink with running water. We did not have an indoor bathroom. We had what you called an *outhouse* or a *johnny house*. We had to use the bathroom outside in that outhouse.

The beauty of the outhouse, which I thought, was that the outhouse had two holes inside of it side by side so that two people can at least use the outhouse at the same time. I thought that was something special because no one else in the neighborhood had two holes in their outhouses. However, I do not recall ever having company while I was in there doing my business. One hole would have been sufficient but, since there were eight of us in the house, two holes made more sense just in case someone really had to use the outdoor bathroom badly.

One of my biggest fears about the outhouse was that I would fall into the hole with the human waste in it. I did not fall into the hole in the outhouse. However, one of my cousins from New Jersey had an unforgettable incident in the outhouse. My cousin was raised in New Jersey and had never seen an outhouse before. He was raised in a home that had an indoor bathroom. While visiting us in the country, he had to relieve himself and was grossed out that he had to use the outhouse. Well, he did his business in the outhouse. He had his wallet in his back pocket, and his wallet fell down on top of the human waste. He was devastated and freaked out. My brother was able to retrieve the wallet with a stick and remove the contents. The wallet was discarded, as my cousin no longer wanted the wallet. Could you blame him?

My other fear was that a snake would crawl up through the hole in the outhouse and pop my butt. I would never sit over the hole but would squat while doing my business (TMI). While in the outhouse, I was always observing my surroundings to make sure that if there was a snake lurking around somewhere that I would see it before it saw me. Thank goodness that there was never a snake as far as I knew of.

CHAPTER 1

Spiritual Bondage

Spiritual bondage is the state of being spiritually bound so that you cannot function or live the way you were designed to function and live (Freedomnowministries).

Growing up, everything seemed normal, except me to a degree. You see, I grew up living in fear of everything: fear of life, fear of death, fear of rejection. I would not speak to people first because I was afraid and would be embarrassed if they did not speak back. One area in which I learned fear was in the church. My family and I were members of a Pentecostal church, whom I love dearly. Let me be clear. My upbringing in the church helped shape me into who I am today, be it spiritually, emotionally, or mentally. I am not speaking against anyone's teaching or preaching. The preacher apparently did his job. I was too afraid to sin. I am just sharing my life's experiences and how they affected me, beginning with my childhood into adulthood.

One of the things that I remembered vividly were the sermons preached. They were about the world coming to an end and going to hell. Preached about going to hell if you drink alcohol, going to hell if you smoked, going to hell if you shacked up, going to hell if——. Hell was embedded in my brain. While writing this book, I had a conversation with my daughter regarding the topics of my book. She remembered when we went to church, and the preacher preached about hell. She was terrified. When she got home, she called her dad to let him know that he was going to hell if he did not get his life right. She was a child. I understood how it frightened her. As a child, it scared the hell out of me. I was terrified of God. I was terrified to make a mistake. I felt that I had to be a perfect child to go to heaven. I was so terrified that I did not want to go out of the house. I felt that if the world ended that I would be safe because I was in an enclosed environment. I did not play outside a lot like my siblings because I was afraid, especially if the skies looked dark or stormy. I was afraid because it was said that Jesus was coming back on a cloud. I felt that He was coming back to get me but not in a good way.

I remembered one day my mom was washing clothes. I was lingering around the washing machine. Back in that day, this was a washing machine with the wringer, the one that you had to pull the clothes through. Not that the type of washing machine mattered, but the point is that I was hanging around in the house on a sunny day. My mom said to me, "Why don't you go outside and play with the other children?" I hesitated, but I went outside. I had no excuse to stay indoors on a sunny day. If only my mom knew how terrified I was to go outside. If she only knew my fear. If she only knew how messed up in my head I was as a child. The constant reminder of going to hell had affected me physically, spiritually, and mentally. I took everything literally. It was hard trying to dot every "i" and cross every "t." I was determined to do good.

At one point, my sister called me Goody Two-Shoes because I did not do wrong. I strived to do the right thing always, whereas my sister stayed in trouble. She had a lot of mouths. She always had something smart to say. She constantly got expelled off of the school bus for talking back to the bus driver. One of her teachers even called her "Motor Mouth" because she was always talking back. My sister used her voice maybe too much when you looked at all the whippings she had gotten.

When I looked at my siblings and how they seemed to be carefree, I wanted to be carefree also. Why is it that they seemed so normal versus myself feeling abnormal? They heard the same messages in church that I did. Did the constant reminder of going to hell affect them? Did they live in fear? Why was I the one to process it with such gloom and doom internally, mentally, and emotionally? I am sure that my siblings will be shocked regarding my mental and emotional state while growing up after reading this book.

No one had any idea how or what I was feeling, especially my parents. I must have had more than the usual childhood sicknesses because I was considered a sickly child. What my parents did not know was that my sickness was more mental. I was paralyzed by fear. I could not function normally. I stayed nervous. My stomach stayed in knots. I was a worrywart. I worried about everything.

In my childhood and teens, my mind stayed in overdrive. It was overloaded with thoughts. I had what is termed *racing thoughts*. It was not so bad in the daytime. However, at night, it prevented me from sleeping. Sometimes I would pretend that I had an eraser in my hand and pretended to erase some of the thoughts away so that my mind could clear. I was in mental pain. My pain was more psychosomatic. In other words, I worried myself sick to the point that it was showing up physically. Whenever someone was sick, I felt their sickness. Being around sickness made me sick. Hearing about someone dying made me felt like I was dying. If I were nervous about something, I would become nauseated and would become physically sick. I would have pains in my stomach, and my mom would sometimes say that maybe it was ulcers. It was said when I was a child that ulcers came from worrying. Maybe my mom knew to the degree that I was a worrier. I supposed she recognized my symptoms, as she too was the nervous type and a worrier. I guess you can say that I inherited the nervousness and worrying from my mother. I had her DNA. I guess she had her own story.

Whenever any of us kids were sick or had pain, my mom would always take us to the doctor. If I did have physical pain, I usually thought that I was dying. I don't know why I felt like I was going to die. Death was constantly on my mind. Whenever I had pain, I would say to myself that that must be "the day" that I was going to die. At the end of the day, I was still alive. This was my thought process into early adulthood. Why have I never told anyone? It was because I felt that if I complained, I was not being perfect. I was not a complainer. I was an introvert. All my feelings, good or bad, were bottled up inside of me.

Living in fear was a horrible feeling. It was traumatizing. Living a life thinking about death and going to hell constantly was miserable and exhausting. Each day I lived my life saying, "If I die today, I am going to hell." I said that daily, even throughout my midtwenties. I tried to be conscientious about being a good girl. I did not drink or cuss. Well, I had drunk only one beer in my lifetime. I was afraid to drink alcohol. I felt that if I died, I wanted to stand before the Lord with nothing in my system. I wanted to be clean in His presence.

I have said a few choice words occasionally. Who hasn't? Those choice words were not part of my vocabulary and did not even sound right coming from me. Not that I was too good to cuss, but I did not hear choice words growing up in my household as a child. Even as an adult, choice words were not used in our home. It just was not part of our vocabulary. When I was younger, I remembered seeing this pretty lady at the laundromat. She cussed her small child out for whatever reason. My heart ached for that child. I could only imagine what she said to him at home. It made her looked so ugly regardless of how pretty she was. I did not know her but have seen her around town occasionally. To this day, whenever I see her, I still remember how her words affected me even though her words were not directed at me.

CHAPTER 2

Contemplated Suicide

I had always considered myself a "mature child" because I did not play a lot like the other kids. I was mature emotionally for my age. I had great responsibilities as a child. I was the one that everyone looked up to in my teen years and even now. I was the one that everyone would come to problem solve. I was the one that everyone knew they could depend on. I was the one who had good grades and could help my siblings with homework. When our parents went into town, I was the one to make sure the house was clean before our parents returned so that we would not get in trouble. I was the one in charge. Once I started driving, I had even greater responsibilities. When I think about it, I did not have my own identity. I was whoever anyone needed me to be. I was a people pleaser. I did not say no because I did not want to hurt anyone's feelings. It did not matter that my feelings were hurt, so I felt at that time. I cared more for others than I did myself, even to the point of protecting my predator, which I will reveal later in the story.

One of the things we were taught in a holiness church was that women should not wear makeup or pants or cut their hair. When I got to middle school, I felt like I had stepped into the Twilight Zone. Girls had on mini-skirts, makeup, and revealing tight clothes. I went from a black-and-white world to a world of living color. I believed my eyes popped open wide, and my mouth dropped open. The culture in the city was so much different from the culture in the country. I tried to adapt. One time I wore a mini-skirt, and I felt totally uncomfortable. I was not brought up to wear clothes like that. I began to notice that the girls in the city did not look like me. Rather, I did not look like them. They had big boobs, big legs, and big butts. I had none of those things. I was a scrawny kid with no shape whatsoever. I had compared myself to the size and shape of a pencil—thin and shapeless.

I had begun to feel that something was wrong with me. I did not look like them. I had begun to despise my looks. I had become super insecure. I felt worthless. On top of that, I was super shy. I started to hate myself. I hated how I looked in the mirror. I remembered looking into the mirror, putting red lipstick on just to be like them. I didn't even like that look. I was hurting, feeling the pain deep within. I took that red lipstick and drew it all over my face like you would see a deranged person in a horror movie. I hated myself. Around that same time, I began to have suicidal thoughts. I took a knife and put it on my wrist. After feeling the cold blade on my wrist, I put the knife away simply because I did not like pain. Too, we were told as a child that if someone committed suicide, they were going to hell. I was already scared of hell. I now know that statement is not scriptural.

The pain not only came from my low self-esteem, but I had no self-esteem. I was burdened with secrets: mine and other folks' secrets. My family is not aware of this to this day, but I was constantly sexually assaulted by an older family friend. Whenever we were alone, I had to fight him off of me. I was about fifteen years old. I told no one, not even my parents. I did not tell because I felt that my daddy would kill that person. If my daddy had harmed that person, I would have felt guilty with his blood on my hands. So I had to protect that person. No self-esteem plus sexual assaults equaled increased suicidal thoughts. The burden of those secrets was heavy on me as a child. I could not tell anyone that I did not want to be left alone with that person. I continued to suffer in silence. I had to act normal whenever in that person's presence, whatever normal was.

My dad had a farm with a tobacco crop. We worked in the summer, from handling the tobacco leaves to driving the tractor to hashing tobacco in the barn. Everyone pitched in. My dad paid us whenever the crop was sold. My friends used to be amazed that our dad would pay us when the crop was sold. That was how we were able to buy our own school clothes. My dad loved farming. Even after everyone moved away from home, my dad continued to farm.

When my mom worked in tobacco, she would fix lunch for us. After lunch, everyone would go back to the tobacco bench or tobacco field, even her. After my mom started to work a public job, I was left with the task of preparing lunch for everyone. After everyone ate lunch, I had to go back to the tobacco bench or tobacco field like everyone else. I felt like I had double duty, which I did. I did not mind in the beginning because I was used to being there for everyone and doing whatever was expected of me. I was used to accomplishing whatever was before me. I was a doer and still am a doer.

After a while, I remembered feeling over-whelmed and even more suicidal. My dad would send me into the city to pick up supplies for the farm. I was sixteen years old by then and had my driver's license. I remembered driving and feeling very overwhelmed. While the car was still going down the road, I laid down across the front seat, attempting suicide. I remembered the car running off the shoulder of the road, but then I sat up and took hold of the steering wheel. I went into town to get the supplies like nothing ever happened. I did not really want to die. I just wanted the pain to go away.

> I shall not die but live and declare
> the works of the Lord. (Psalm 118:17
> KJV)

No one ever knew that took place. Until now. Thank God for His angels encamped around me even though I did not know it at that time.

Apparently, I was not the only family member who had suicidal thoughts. In 1996, my brother, who was one year older than me, committed suicide. He and I were very close. People thought we were twins in high school. In every homeroom, I would sit in the seat in front of him because of our alphabetical names. He had failed the sixth grade; therefore, we were in the same grades and graduated high school together. One night when we were still living at home, my brother went out with some friends. That night when he came home, he was not acting his normal self. He was hallucinating. It was after midnight, so we had to sneak him through the window into the house. My dad's rule was that if we were not home by midnight, we would not get in. Because of my brother's behavior, we had to wake our dad to let him know that something was wrong with our brother. My parents got up and took him to the hospital. He had gotten ahold of "something" that affected his overall well-being. He was okay. However, my dad thinks to this day that somehow that night affected my brother's mental health as an adult.

At some point in his adult life, he was diagnosed with Schizophrenia. He had a young family and was very overwhelmed. He was receiving medications to help maintain mental stability. At that time, I was not working in the medical field. Therefore, I was not aware of the symptoms of Schizophrenia. I only knew he was in mental turmoil. He would walk and talk in slow motion. I attributed his actions to the disease. Now that I work in the medical field, I know now that it was the medication that had my brother in a zombie-like state. My brother would make suicidal statements often, but at the same time, he always told me that he would never harm himself because he had four young boys and a daughter depending on him. I felt relieved knowing that he had a motivating factor to live. He gave me his gun to keep to make sure he did not have a weapon to harm himself. Whenever he felt overwhelmed, like he was not going to make it, he always called me. Always. I would get off work and go wherever he was. I was able to calm him and give him hope.

On the day that he committed suicide, he was not able to get ahold of me. I had switched jobs. Apparently, he did not have my new work number. I am pretty certain that he tried to reach me. I received the dreadful phone call that I needed to come to my brother's house. My mom and I worked at the same place. I had to go pick her up. She kept asking me on the way to my brother's house if I thought it was true that my brother, her son, was gone. I did not answer because I did not want to believe it. I felt in my heart that he was gone. However, I was not going to share my fears with my mom.

When we reached his home, the funeral director was there and had already put him in the hearse. The pain was indescribable. Even now, as I am writing this part, my tears are flowing. My heart still aches for him and his children. I felt partly responsible for his death. I missed the signs. I really thought my brother was getting better. About two weeks before his death, he perked up. He was happier. He paid up his bills in advance. He shaved his head. I thought he had a new lease on life. He came back for his gun. I gave it back to him because he seemed to be thriving. In fact, it was the opposite. When I realized that the weapon he used to kill himself was the weapon that I gave back to him, I was a total mess. I felt guilty as if I had pulled the trigger myself. One thing I will always remember is that although he talked of suicide, he always asked God for forgiveness. Always. It was a daily mantra for him to ask God constantly throughout the day for forgiveness.

That was super hard for me. I could not eat from the time my brother died until the time he was buried. I lost so much weight in those three days. My clothes just hung on me. They were too big due to the extreme weight loss. His death was devastating for our family. My mom and dad were in no shape to plan his funeral. I took the reign and planned his funeral. I wrote the obituary and assigned certain ones to participate in the church service. My brother was dearly loved. If he only knew. As we were driving out to the cemetery, I remembered looking behind us just to see the extremely long procession honoring his life. That made me smile to see the love that was shown for him and my family. When I think about it now, I wonder if he had suicidal tendencies while growing up as I did.

Suicidal ideation still existed in my family. I will not reveal this family member's name. This individual spoke about suicide if———. This statement was made on several occasions. I finally told that family member that it would be a selfish thing to do if such an act was committed. I reminded that family member how devastated the family was when we lost our brother to suicide. I reminded that family member how we are still dealing with the aftermath of our brother's death. I assured that family member that things would be okay and that there was no reason to worry if———. After that day, that family member no longer brought up the subject of suicide. That conversation happened about fifteen years ago. That family member is still thriving and surviving. Praise God.

CHAPTER 3

Reconciled with My Father

As mentioned earlier, I felt that I had to be perfect. My attitude was perfect. My grades were perfect. When I turned eighteen, the imperfect person surfaced. I thought I was halfway grown when I turned eighteen. This is my recollection. My sister has a slightly different version. I believe the only difference in our versions is regarding our transportation back home.

You see, on my eighteenth birthday, my dad allowed me and my sister to go out with my male cousin into town at night. His specific instructions were to be home by midnight. My dad was old-school. Even today, he said that if we lived with him that we would still have to be at home by midnight. When we got into town, my sister and I got into separate cars with a couple of male friends. Apparently, time slipped away, and it was nearly 2:00 a.m. My cousin was nowhere in sight and apparently had went home. Therefore, these guys had to take me and my sister home. While en route to home, as we were almost there, we bypassed my dad's car. Apparently, he was going to look for us. When we got home, my dad said angrily, "Y'all gonna get a whipping in the morning! Do y'all know what time it is?"

Now I have to tell you that I was not one to talk back. I was the "good" child. But this night, I said to our dad with a smart mouth, "How do I know? You're the one with the clock in your room!" He made us wash dishes that night. Then he whipped us and sent us to bed.

My sister said to me, "If you hadn't opened your big mouth, we would not have gotten a whipping!" Ironic coming from my sister, right? I had the big mouth this time instead of her. Early that morning, about 6:00 a.m., our dad got up and went outside. I did not know why he went outside so early until he came into our room and pulled the bed covers back. He whipped us again. I did not think we were going to get another whipping since he had whipped us when we got home. I was wrong. I guess he showed me that I was not grown, no matter my age. I remembered that day vividly. I cried the entire day, literally. I had what you called a "hiccup" cry, where I had to catch my breath in between tears. I just made this term up, and it fits my cry perfectly.

That weekend that my sister and I had received our whipping was actually the last weekend that we spent together as a family. The very morning of our whipping, my mom and dad separated. My mom moved me and my sister to the city to my grandmother's home. My brothers stayed in the country with my dad. My mom did not like for us to get whippings. She made up excuses for us. When my parents separated, I felt that it was my fault since I had cried the entire day of the whipping. That guilt overwhelmed me for many years, feeling that I was the reason they had separated. I knew that they had their own issues in the relationship. However, since they separated on the day I received my whipping, I associated the separation based on the whipping incident. I was in my senior year of high school, which made it even tougher.

Once we moved to the city, my personality changed. I went from being a scared little girl to being a daring teenager. I became friends with a city girl who was daring, whom I learned these behaviors from. I ended up skipping school. I stole fruit off the salad bar. Not that I was hungry, but it was a dare. It felt good being a bad girl for a change instead of doing what was right all the time. I started having anger issues. I was angry at my dad. I was angry at the world. There was no sunshine in my life. All I saw was darkness. When people used to say good morning, my words or my thought process was, *What is so good about it?*

My anger turned into bitterness. I remembered trying to open a can of luncheon meat. The key on the can twisted. I could not use the key anymore. I tried to pull the can apart with my hands. The edges were sharp. I knew that I was going to cut my hand. I didn't care. I kept pulling on the can. Sure enough, the can cut my hand. There was a lot of blood. My mom was not home. I ran to the neighbor's house. She took me to the hospital. I had to have stitches on my right thumb. I knew then that if I continued going down the path of destruction with my *I-don't-care* attitude that worse things would happen to me. Well, at least I no longer had suicidal ideations.

I am not sure how long it was before I saw my dad again after the separation. He would stop by occasionally to check on me and my sister. About two years later, after the separation, he helped me get a part-time job where he worked. We would ride to work together because I did not have transportation. We began to communicate more. It was not until after my brother had died, which was several years later, that I eventually worked up the nerve to ask him if I was the reason that he and my mom had separated. He told me that I was not the reason. I kind of knew it, but it felt good to hear my dad say that it was not my fault. By that time, I had my own family. I wanted him to be a part of my family. So I had to ask that hard question because I did not want to continue to suffer in silence.

Many years after I had married and had children, my dad and I recounted the story of my last whipping at age eighteen to my children, who were preteens. My children were shocked that I had gotten a whipping at age eighteen. My dad told them that if he thought I needed a whipping today that he would give me a whipping. My children looked at me and said, "Ma, you would let Granddaddy whip you?"

I said, "Well, he is my daddy."

My dad then said, "I don't think she needs a whipping. I think she's been good." Then we all laughed. Even though I was halfway grown when I received my last whipping, I appreciated the whippings. It helped shaped me into the adult that I am today—respectful, caring, advocate, giving, nurturing. The whippings were our parents' way of showing us love and keeping us grounded to prevent us from getting into trouble in life. It worked.

To this day, my dad and I have a great relationship. In times past, he would accompany me to my doctor's appointment, especially if I didn't want my mom to know because she would worry and stress about what could be wrong with me. I would also accommodate him to his appointments. My dad is now eighty-one years old. He is totally blind after an unsuccessful eye surgery in 2019. He is dependent on his family for everything. I know that it is frustrating for him because he has lost a lot of his independence. He had always said that he never wanted to rely on people for anything.

I reminded him that he and my mom took care of us when we were kids and could not take care of ourselves, and now it is time for us to take care of him. He gets discouraged sometimes because he sees total darkness on a daily basis. That would make anyone discouraged. Another eye surgery is pending. I tell him often that I am believing God for a miracle to restore his vision. I believe that my dad will see again. If Jesus can heal blind Bartimaeus, Saul who persecuted Christians and was struck blind by a light from heaven, and the man blind since birth whose parents did not sin, surely He is still a healer today and can heal my dad.

CHAPTER 4

Being Violated

I am not sure when I started feeling this way or why in my childhood, but I struggled with needing to be "loved." I was desperate for love. I was the one that needed to hear it. Why? I do not know. Did any of my siblings feel this way? I knew that my parents loved me and us. There were no doubts of that. I think in reality, I just did not love myself. I needed validation from others to fill that void. My parents were from the generation that they did not tell each other that they loved each other. I never heard my parents say "I love you" to each other. I knew that they did. Our home growing up was full of love, though not said. My parents showed their love in every way. We lacked nothing. We were a happy family. I was the one with the problem. It affected me terribly.

Throughout my life, I needed validation. I needed to feel self-worth. I needed reassurance. I was needy. In my second marriage, we told each other and our children constantly that we loved them. I wanted to make sure that love was manifested in our home. I did not want our children to ever question if we loved them or not. Even to this day, just about every time we talk, we always say we love each other. We may talk two or three times a day sometimes, and we always end with "I love you."

I was determined that they would feel our love. The love that our children had received transferred to my parents, their grandparents. Our children would tell my parents that they love them. My parents would say it back. I was overjoyed because my kids received from my parents what I had longed for: to hear those words, "I love you." Since our kids opened that door of expressing love to my parents, I was able to sneak in my little "I love you," and my parents would say it back. That generational curse was broken. That gap was filled. I see it today in my siblings and their families. We all say we love each other. God's love is the greatest love. The next best love is my love for myself. I no longer need validation. I now know who I am.

I remembered things changed for me when I went to middle school. Elementary school was my years of innocence, except the last summer before middle school. This guy and I called ourselves boyfriend and girlfriend. One summer night, my siblings and I went over to my boyfriend's house. He and I went off by ourselves. We ended up having sex. We had no clue what we were doing. I was so distraught that I thought I was pregnant that same night. I had made myself physically sick that same night. I could not eat food. To look at it or smell it made me sick. I was more sick of guilt and shame for what had happened. I could not tell anybody. My aunt had come down from New Jersey. She noticed that I was sick and throwing up. She made the comment, "I hope you are not pregnant like your other cousin in New Jersey." I could not say anything because I did not know the answer to that. I did not know what it meant to be pregnant. I did not know what sex was about. Things like that were not discussed in our household. We were sheltered as kids.

I was traumatized by that experience. The guilt and shame were overwhelming. I had sinned. I knew I was hell-bound now. I could not share with anyone because I was too scared. I did not want anyone to be disappointed in me. After that, I did not engage in any sexual activity for a year. There is a saying that women hear is that, "If he is not getting it from you, he is getting it from somebody." I decided to try it again with the same boyfriend.

This time around, the experience was not so bad. I actually enjoyed the experience. One reason that I continued to engage in sexual activity was that it was the only time that I felt loved or happy. The more I engaged in sexual activity, the more loved and happier I felt. It was the only time that I felt good about myself. So I continued to have sex. Outside of sex, I felt empty. I felt numb. I was self-medicating with sex. I did not feel violated with this sexual encounter. It was my choice, my way of coping. Well, the world did not end after my wrongdoings. It took me years before I dabbled in worldly things in my teen years. I was too afraid because I did not want to go to hell. As each year passed, I realized that although I had done wrong, Christ had not come. I did believe He was coming though. As time went on, I would continue to test the waters and do something that I was not supposed to do. Yet, although I tested the waters, I still said to myself that if I died that day, I would go to hell. So I was not comfortable doing wrong.

After high school, I called myself venturing out, stepping into deeper waters. I had a couple of one-night stands. I just did not get the hype. I knew the guys but did not have a relationship with them. Sex was meaningless, no emotions, no joy or pleasure for me with them. There were no connections for me. I quickly nipped that in the bud. As Barney Fife said on the Andy Griffin show, "Nip it, nip it, nip it." I realized how women could get attached to men so easily.

This is my theory. When having sex, the man makes his deposit inside of a woman. She can bathe, shower, etc., and still, he is inside of her. She goes to work, he's inside her. She goes to bed, he's inside her. His excretion is attached to her. Whereas the man, he can cleanse himself and keep it moving. He does not walk around with her secretion on him. He can walk away easily. Or he can go back and make another deposit.

The Holy Spirit just placed this in my spirit about a safety deposit box. Women should treat their bodies like a safety deposit box. Inside of a safety deposit box are things of value, things you find worthy, things worth safe keeping. In order to get inside of a safety deposit box, you have to have two keys. The owner of the safety deposit box gets a key, and one other person gets a key. It takes two identical keys to open a safety deposit box. If the man has the other key, he cannot get into your safety deposit box unless you give him your key. If his key does not match your key, then he cannot get into your safety deposit box. If he is not depositing anything of value into your life, why give him a key?

If he continues to make withdrawals and not depositing fruit into your life, why give him a key? Everything in that safety deposit box is something that you worked hard to hold on to, that is why it is in the safety deposit box for safe keeping. Beloved, you are a precious keepsake. You are a treasure. Do not allow anyone to continue to make counterfeit deposits into your life. Exodus 19:5 (NKJV) says:

> Now therefore, if you will
> indeed obey My voice and keep My

covenant, then ye shall be a special
treasure to Me above all people; for
all the earth is Mine.

We belong to God. All that we have belongs to
God. Set guard around your safety deposit box. Just
as the Holy Spirit deposited this good word into me
to give you, cherish your treasures. Protect it. You
are worth more than how someone makes you feel
in or out of bed.

After I realized that I was violating my body
by giving it away, I began to have better respect for
myself. I set up boundaries with males. I kept both
keys to my safety deposit box until I decided who
earned a key. My decision, not theirs. Of course, I
was not saved then. I was not in His Word. I was
committing fornication (consensual sexual inter-
course between two persons not married to each
other).

Ephesians 5:3 (NKJV) says:

But fornication, and all
uncleanness, or covetousness, let it
not be named among you, as is fit-
ting for saints.

Romans 12:1–2 (NIV) tells us to present our
bodies as a living sacrifice, holy and pleasing to God.
This is your true and proper worship. Again, every-

thing that we have belongs to God, especially our bodies. Our bodies are a temple. God cannot dwell in an unclean temple. We must glorify Him with our bodies.

While I am on the subject of violation, a violator tried to take away the keys to my safety deposit box. Once again, I was sexually assaulted. During this time, my sister and I were the only ones living in my grandmother's house in the city. My grandmother had gotten remarried and left the house to my mother. My mother had moved out, so my sister and I lived there. This particular time, I believe it was my sister's friends who were over in the middle of the night playing cards. The friends were leaving, and my sister went to bed. I had prepared for bed when there was a knock at the front door. I thought maybe one of her friends had forgotten something, so I let him in. As soon as he entered the room, he threw me onto the bed.

The bedroom was located to the right once you walk in the front door. He was on top of me trying to take off my clothes. I was fighting him off of me. I was screaming at the top of my lungs. I kept screaming. Finally, my sister came out of the back room. When she came into where the perpetrator and I were, the guy jumped up and ran out the front door. Had my sister not entered the room, he would have raped me. I am so thankful that my sister finally heard my plea for help.

When I think about what happened to me, I truly believe that this guy has done this before to other women or girls. He has violated other females. I did not file a police report because I was scared and ashamed. I did not think that they would believe me. I did not know him but only knew of him. I could not pick him out of a lineup even today. That is how much I did not know him and would not have been able to identify him. I knew he had several brothers who looked alike, and I did not want to take the chance of choosing the wrong person. Therefore, I did not report the incident.

According to statistics from the NISVS 2015 Data Brief: Sexual Violence by any Perpetrator, "approximately one in five (21.3 percent or an estimated 25.5 million) women in the US reported complete or attempted rape at some point in their lifetime. A majority of female victims of completed or attempted rape first experienced such victimization early in life, with 81.3 percent (nearly 20.8 million victims) reporting that it first occurred prior to age twenty-five." I was amazed when I read the statistics, as I was 23 years old when I was sexually assaulted.

I know firsthand how scary it is to report being violated. One Sunday after church while shopping at Walmart with my children, I was violated once again. I was looking at clothes on the rack. There were a top layer of clothes and a bottom layer of clothes. These were children clothes. While looking at the top layer, I felt a brush of wind beneath me. There happened to be a man on his knees looking up my dress. When I looked down at him, he shifted his position as if he was looking at the clothes. I shook my head in disbelief. I kept saying to myself, *I know that did not just happen.* I kept playing that scene over in my mind while still in the store. I had contemplated whether to report it or not. The guy was of a different race. I did not report it because I felt that the manager would not believe me. I took my kids and left the store. This was one time that I wished I had flatulence. Okay, gas. Instead of me reporting him to the police, he would have reported me for having a deadly weapon in public.

After I returned home, I asked myself, *What if that had happened to my children? What would my advice be to them?* My advice would be to report the pervert. Well, I did not take my own advice. I regretted not reporting the incident. To halfway make it right, the next day I went back to Walmart. I reported the incident. The police was called. I gave my statement. I didn't think about it at the time, but Walmart had cameras. I am not sure if the policeman pulled the cameras. Had I reported it earlier, the cameras would have been my evidence. We tell our children that if anyone touches them inappropriately to tell someone. Imagine how frightening it would have been if this had happened to a child.

Would they have told someone? Here I am an adult, and it was frightening for me to tell someone who could have intervened. With that said and with everything going on in society today, please keep your children in eyesight and arm's length when out in public.

This subject that I am about to discuss was a topic that I struggled with. I struggled because I feel that this is the most personal subject to reveal. I violated myself. One reason that I am revealing this is because someone out there is struggling with the choice that they have made. They continue to condemn themselves for this mistake. They need to know that God will and has forgiven them if they asked. He has already sent this burden into the sea of forgetfulness, not the sea of remembrance. Now they need to forgive themselves. I share this because someone needs healing and deliverance from the aftermath of their decision. The subject that I am sharing is that I aborted a pregnancy. Yes, I had an abortion in my early twenties. I made that decision. I have to be honest and say that this subject was not one that I terribly struggled with when it happened. I had to look at all areas of my life emotionally, mentally, spiritually, physically, and the affect the pregnancy would have had in my unstable life. I did not care for the person whom I was semi-involved with. It was just something to do. With that said, I made a decision that was best for me.

I am not proud of it, but I do not beat myself up about it either. God has forgiven me. I have forgiven myself. You may say, "Oh, she's telling all her business." No, I am not telling all of my business. I am sharing my journey, my truth, my testimony in hopes that someone will be healed and delivered from this past burden. Therefore, my sharing is not in vain.

Beloved, you can go forward with your head up high with a smile on the inside as well as the outside knowing that God does not hold your past against you.

> If we confess our sins, He is faithful and just to forgive us our sins and to cleanse us from all unrighteousness. (1 John 1:9 NKJV)

Psalm 103:10–12 (ESV) tells us that, "God has not dealt with us according to our sins, nor repay us according to our iniquities. For as high as the heavens are above the earth, so great is His steadfast love toward those who fear him; as far as the east is from the west, so far does he remove our transgressions from us."

It's like my bishop says, "You can't drive a car forward looking in the rearview mirror." Try it and let me know how it works for you. It will not work. To reach your destiny, you have to keep it moving forward. An ex of mine once said, "Your past is like your behind (well, he used another word). That is where it is at, and there is where it will always be—behind you."

CHAPTER 5

Domestic Violence

Although this chapter is true, it has been tweaked some in order to share my truth only and no one else's truth. As I began to write this chapter, all of a sudden, I felt emotional. Tears began to flow down my face. Why? It has been almost forty years since the abuse. I am over it, aren't I? I did not know anything about domestic violence or abuse. I grew up in a sheltered home. We were protected and felt safe. We did not know that there was a world out there that we needed to be protected from.

This guy and I were just friends. For me, there was no chemistry. He knew where I worked. He used to ask to pick me up from work and take me home, but I constantly refused. I did not have a car at that time, so I had to catch a ride wherever I went. It was summertime, and everyone was hanging out and going to the lake, except me. I was bored one day, and this guy asked me to go to the lake. I said yes just to be doing something. I knew that this guy had a girlfriend. I was not trying to come between them. I just wanted to go to the lake. It was fun riding around and seeing everyone out. I kind of liked it but still not necessarily feeling him. However, I continued to accept rides to the lake and other outings.

One day this guy told me that he had broken up with his girlfriend. I had asked, "Why did you do that?" He said that he wanted to be with me. I told him he shouldn't have done that because I was not trying to be in a relationship. I wanted to just have fun hanging out. Eventually, I continued to hang out with this guy, and we became intimate. It was like a different kind of relationship. Whatever I asked for, he gave it to me. He did not deny me anything. He treated me like a queen. But what I did not know was that there would be a hefty price to pay for the royal treatment later in the relationship.

I knew that this guy was possessive and jealous and was used to having his way. The first time I had experienced domestic abuse was during a Christmas holiday season. We had gone to Kmart to pick up presents for my family. At that time, I was no longer working. I relied on this guy for my needs and wants. After we parked and got out of the car, I was a few steps ahead of him. As I was preparing to go inside Kmart, a guy coming out of Kmart was holding the door open for me to enter. I entered into the store. The guy that I was with said to me, "That's all right. I'll get you." I did not know what he meant, so I did not pay any attention to that statement. I proceeded to eat my chocolate chip ice cream cone that we had purchased before we got to the store. I also proceeded to pick out gifts for my family, which he paid for.

Once we were in the back of the store at Kmart, he smacked me in my face. I was stunned and hurt because I didn't understand why he hit me. Needless to say, I held on to my ice cream cone and the items that we were going to purchase and headed to the counter. Though I was stunned with tears in my eyes, I was determined to complete the purpose for going to Kmart. When he took me back home, I told him that I did not want to see him again. He became upset and started crying and saying how much he loved me. He begged me and begged me for another chance. I had never seen a man cry like that before. I figured he must have loved me if he was showing that much emotion to not lose me. I reluctantly agreed to continue the relationship.

During the first part of the relationship, he did not hit me again. However, when we were driving and if we had an argument, he would play "chicken" while driving. "Chicken" was when a car is coming toward you on the opposite side of the road and you drive in his lane toward him as if you were going to hit head-on. At the last minute, he jerked the car back in our lane to prevent a head-on collision. Yes, it scared the daylights out of me, but I deep down did not think he was crazy enough to kill us. When I think about it now, he did not love me or himself to jeopardize his life, my life, and innocent lives.

Eventually, we cohabited. There still was no chemistry for me. Again, it was just something to do. Besides at that time, my parents had separated. My sister and I had moved into the city with our mom. We had plenty of room, but then two of my brothers began staying regularly. I was sleeping on the couch. After this guy that I was dating asked me to move in with him, I accepted the offer, mainly because I was tired of sleeping on the couch. I wanted my own room. It sounded like a good idea at that time. Right? Not!

Shortly afterward, my world turned upside down. The relationship went from me getting everything I wanted to getting nothing that I wanted. After he got what he wanted, which was me, things changed. He no longer gave me money. He took the keys to the cars away from me. He took the phone out of the home when he went to work so that I could not contact anyone. We began to argue a lot. He became abusive verbally and physically. He would hit me in areas that were not visible, i.e., upper arm, stomach, thigh. One night while we were fighting, the police showed up at our door. I was sure that the police were going to take him away that night, but they did not. I do not recall if they asked me if I was okay.

When the police left, I felt unsafe. I felt that if the police would do nothing then I had nowhere to turn. I felt hopeless. I had never thought of feeling "unsafe" before even though I felt afraid. Now I felt unsafe. I did not tell anyone in my family what was going on. I was ashamed. I was embarrassed. I thought it would stop. I just continued to suffer in silence.

As time went on, the guy became more controlling. One day we were at a party. We were all sitting around laughing and talking. He said to me, "You better not smile!" By that time, I knew a fight was ensuing. For the heck of it, I smiled anyway. He did not start anything at the party. When we got home, we got into a physical fight. Normally, I would cover my body to protect the blows, but not this time. This time, I started throwing punches and fought back. The scene was like the one in *What's Love Got to Do with It* movie when Angela Bassett, who played Tina Turner, finally had had enough and fought Ike Turner in the back of the limousine. I knew I could not beat him, but he darn well was going to know that he had been in a fight. I was proud of myself that I had some fight in me.

There was this time during the winter when he had turned the heat off in the house to be spiteful. It was so cold in the house that you could actually see your breath. That night when we went to bed, he took all the covers off of me deliberately. I went into the other bedroom to sleep. That bed had light-weight bedcovers on it. I made it through the night. At that point, I grew such hatred for him. I began to think of ways to kill him. Remember, earlier in my book I was suicidal. At this point in my life, I was no longer suicidal. I was thinking homicidal thoughts by now.

One way I had planned to kill him was to set him on fire in the bed when he went to sleep. Of course, the movie *Burning Bed* was out with Farrah Fawcett who played the victim. In that movie, Farrah Fawcett set her husband on fire when he went to sleep. I believed that she went to jail until her case went to trial. I knew that I would not survive in jail one day let alone staying in there until a court date. Therefore, I had to change my plan of thought. I then started preparing a way of escape. I was done. I could not stay in an abusive relationship.

That Monday morning when he left to go to work, I had packed my belongings in a brown paper sack. I called my mom to come get me. He had placed the phone back in the house by then. When he got off work, he saw that I was not home. He knew that I was at my mom's house. He came to my mom's house. He was beyond furious. He was threatening me. A male friend of my mom's was there. He intervened. We threatened to call the police. He left. He sped off fast driving crazy.

Did I go back? Nope. I was done. I deserved better and wanted better. One of the things he had said to me was that I would never make it without him. Those words echoed in my head. I was not determined to prove him wrong, but I was determined to prove me right—that I will survive and succeed on my own. That was when I realized that when someone is buying you literally, it comes with a cost. I paid the price, but I was not willing to pay the interest on it. Lesson learned: Never let someone take care of you for it comes with a price. It may be your life. After I left, he moved away. I never heard from him again. If he could see me now. I achieved an Associate Degree in Medical Office Technology (1992), as well as an Associate Degree in Nursing (RN) in 2005. I was determined to succeed. My greatest accomplishment is accepting Christ Jesus as my Lord and Savior (1990). Because of Him, I was able to reach my goals, including the courage to write this book.

About a year later, I married a high school friend. I was not ready for marriage, but I went through with it anyway. The marriage did not last about a year, give or take six months. I moved out of the home that we had purchased. However, there is a wild memory that I would like to share.

After we bought a home, we started having friends over. One of his cousins in particular was a frequent visitor. We would play cards, and they would drink alcohol. I did not drink alcohol nor did I do drugs, except on this one occasion, which I am about to explain. We were with this couple, and we decided to park in the woods instead of going to our house. While in the woods, we had the light on inside the car. Inside the car, there were opened cans of beer and some marijuana that were going to be shared. Apparently, the neighbors saw a light through the woods and called the police.

While in the process of lighting up, the blue lights and a siren went off behind our car. It was the police. The first thing came to my mind was, *I'm going to jail and I don't even drink beer or smoke weed.* We quickly threw the beer under the seat and hid the marijuana. The policeman walked up to the car. He thought we were there for a rendezvous and told us that we needed to leave from there. It was a good thing that we had not lit up the marijuana because we most likely would have went to jail. We left from there and went back to the house to continue what we had started. That night in our kitchen, I drew a couple of puffs from the reefer. Immediately, I had a headache and went to bed. The others stayed up smoking reefer. I did not see the hype in smoking reefer. I never touched that stuff again.

The beauty of that marriage was that I birthed a beautiful baby girl into the world named Chantel. She was his only child. He adored her immensely. She adored her dad immensely. She definitely was a daddy's girl. Sadly, her world crumbled when she lost her dad in 2008. RIP Fields. Your presence is truly missed.

After my divorce, now I am on my own and have a child to take care of. I went out and got a job. As a matter of fact, I worked two jobs. I worked part-time at the A&P Supermarket and part-time at Revlon. I still did not have a car, so my family would take me to work. I lived approximately seven minutes from A&P Supermarket. I walked most days to work, especially if it was a pretty and sunny day. When it rained, my mom would pick me up from work. I felt pretty good earning my own money. While walking to work, an acquaintance continued to offer me rides from work. I continued to decline. I was satisfied walking to work. After a while, I gave in. We dated for a while. He was a good guy. The only thing was that he wanted to take care of me. Been there, done that, didn't want to do it again. I was not about to let another man take care of me. Lesson learned the hard way the first time. Needless to say, we eventually parted ways.

CHAPTER 6

Confessions

Now I have my own apartment, a car, and a job with the state. I do not have to depend on anyone. Being a single mother had its challenges, but I was determined to make it on my own. If I had a need, I did not ask anyone for anything. At that time, I had a two-year-old daughter. I worked in dietary. Times were tight. There were times when food was low. I made sure she ate what we had at home, and I would eat some of the food where I worked. I applied for food stamps. I was told I made fifty dollars too much. Fifty dollars too much. What's that?

I was determined to make it. I got a second job part-time working at Wendy's. I kept the salad bar clean and prepared. It was okay, but I hated going into the cooler. I did not and still do not like being cold. I didn't stay at that job long. I had applied for a promotion where I worked with the state. I got the job. I quit Wendy's. I was able to take care of my daughter without the struggle. God was still looking out for me even though I did not know it at that time.

After a few months of receiving my promotion, I met my second husband, Russell. I am not proud of how we met, but it is my truth. I do not condone this behavior now. Russell and I met at work. I had interviewed for a job as a Health Care Technician. There were only male staff on that particular unit working with male clients. As I was introduced to the staff during the interview, Russell said that I caught his eye. He was one of the ones to tell the supervisor to hire me. She did.

When I came aboard to work, I worked second shift. Russell worked first shift. By being newly hired, I guess I was fresh meat on the market. The other male staff, about three of them, were very playful and touchy feely playing with me on the job. While the other male staff were playing up on me, I noticed that Russell, the "quiet one" who had convinced the supervisor to hire me, was sitting back "quietly" watching the action. *Huh?* I thought. There is something about the "quiet one" not engaging in the action. Although the male staff were seeing who were going to get me first, they did not know me very well. I don't like pouncers like Tigger on Winnie the Pooh. I like the subtle type. I like to see who you are gradually, not all at once.

Russell admitted later that he was stewing, watching the other male staff vying for my attention when in fact he liked me. To this day, he can still tell you what I wore to the interview over thirty years ago: black sweater, royal blue and black checkered pants, and loafer shoes with a penny in it. Yes, he had to be smitten to remember those details.

As Russell and I continued to work together, we formed a friendship. One of his male coworkers pointed out to him that I was eyeing him on the side like I was interested in him. That gave Russell the courage to approach me. We enjoyed seeing each other at work. We had so much conversation and laughter. Things were beginning to change for us. Our conversations were lasting longer. Our conversations were getting more personal. He finally asked to take me out. I declined. Not that I didn't want to go out with him, but I had a good reason.

He and I were both engaged to other people. He was engaged to his high school sweetheart. They had been together for about ten years. My fiancé and I had been together maybe about two years. Both our pasts showed a history of cheating. We had agreed not to pursue a relationship because we did not want to continue that pattern of cheating. We wanted to remain "faithful" to our then partners. We remained friends on the job. A couple of months went by, and it was my birthday. Russell wanted to give me a birthday kiss on the job. I agreed. What did I do that for? I was hooked. I had not expected such a kiss for it took me to another dimension. After the kiss, I still did not want to pursue a relationship, although my mind and heart were truly wandering.

One night while I was at my apartment, Russell showed up unexpectedly. We talked a bit. When he got ready to leave, he asked for a kiss. After that kiss, it was undeniable that we had great chemistry. Actually we had great chemistry before the kiss, but the kiss confirmed our chemistry. We totally connected. After this second kiss, he told me later in the relationship that he said to himself, *Um, I got her now.* And he did.

It was a wonderful romance. We worked different shifts. We would leave love notes on the job for one another in the adjoining bathroom behind a clipboard. He would find the note when he came to work that morning. I would find one from him behind that clipboard in the evening. We would stay up all hours of the night talking sometimes to about 5:00 a.m. By then, it was time for him to get up at 6:00 a.m. to go to work. I would feel bad for him, but when I saw him when I got to work, he looked refreshed and not tired from staying up all night. I felt guilty because I knew of his fiancée. I actually liked her as a person. I did not feel guilty enough to stop. For once, I got to choose who to love instead of being chosen.

I stayed over often at Russell's apartment as if he did not have a fiancée. We continued the romance even though we both had fiancées. So there were four of us in a relationship. One of the things that made it tolerable for me was that I felt safe with him. He encouraged me to grow. He always told me how funny and smart I was and that I had a good head on my shoulders. He made me feel that I was deserving of happiness, deserving of love.

One day my then-fiancé, my daughter, and I were at the lake. Russell was there with his then-fiancée also. This was not planned. He and his fiancée were cooking on the grill. He had on a chef's apron with the chef's tools in his hand looking liked he knew what he was doing. He looked like a grill master. I looked over there and said to myself, *Dawg, I wish I had a man who cooked on the grill!* My thought shifted when my daughter wanted to swing near where Russell and his then-fiancée were grilling. We both were relieved when my daughter did not notice them. Russell and I said when we met up later that day, we were afraid that my daughter was going to call out to him and then we both would have some explaining to do as to how my daughter knew him. Oh, by the way, Russell said that was the first time he had ever grilled. He looked like he had been doing it all the time.

Another first for him that he shared was when we went to Myrtle Beach. I remembered asking him only once to go to the beach. He made it happened immediately. Whereas I had been asking my then fiancé to go, and we never went to the beach. To think that Russell honored my request without hesitation even though we were engaged to other people was mind blowing to me. That was when he won my heart. I thought that he was accustomed to going to beach on whims when he admitted that actually that was his first time going to the beach as well. I really felt special then.

After a while, I could not pretend to love my then-fiancé any longer and ended the relationship. But before we ended the relationship, I got caught. Russell and I were lying in bed one early Monday morning. He had to get up to go to work. At five in the morning, we heard music blasting loud out in the parking lot. We both looked at each other and said, "That's my fiancé." Sure enough, it was. When I peeped out the window, my then-fiancé was getting out of the car. Russell jumped out of the bed, grabbed his clothes, and ran out the back door in the rain. Needless to say, he later caught a cold.

My fiancé entered the house and asked me what I was doing up so early. I heed and hawed. He told me that he recognized Russell's car outside. I confessed. We argued. It was the perfect excuse to break up. After the breakup, now we were down to three in the relationship. Whenever Russell and I hear the song "As We Lay" by Shirley Murdock, it brings us back to this memory, as well as Secret Lovers. I have to give myself a little credit. I was honest with my fiancé at the time. I told him that I wanted to go out with Russell. He objected, of course. I told him I was going anyway because I was tired of people making decisions for me. I wanted to create my own happiness for a change.

After a while longer, I decided that I no longer wanted to share Russell. I expressed that to him. He was willing to let go of his ten-year relationship. He had quite a bit of reservations because he only knew me for a short time compared to knowing his fiancée for years. I understood that. He knew of my cheating history, whereas his fiancée never cheated on him. It was kind of like the good versus the bad. The romance went on with the three of us until he could make a clean break from his ten-year relationship. The break was not that clean. We got caught.

One Saturday evening, Russell and I had gone to the strawberry patch to pick berries. We came back to his apartment. I made a strawberry pie. While the pie was in the oven, the doorbell rang. It was his fiancée. She entered into the apartment. We greeted each other politely.

I could see the hurt in her eyes. She asked to speak to him in the bedroom. I stayed in the kitchen. After a while, I went to check on them in the bedroom. She was upset and rightfully so. I empathized with her. I said to her, "I know how you feel. I dated a guy for eight years, and I thought we would get married and did not. I know you love Russell, but I love him too."

His fiancée asked him to make a choice that night. He chose me. I was shocked but well pleased. He told me that he chose me for several reasons: there was something about my eyes that drew him in, my outgoing personality, the way I wanted something out of life, and that I had a good head on my shoulders. To this day, I still think fondly of his ex-fiancée. I have even said that if we were not in competition for the same guy, that I would not have mind being friends. Nevertheless, I sincerely apologize now for infringing on their relationship. I vowed after that to never do that to another woman.

Now there were two of us. We made a vow that because of our history of cheating on our partners that if there were ever a third party coming between us, that would be the end of our relationship. We were trying to build trust. I let him know from the get-go that if he was to play me, that I would play him harder. Again, it was a great romance. One year later in the relationship, I had become pregnant with our son, Russell Jr a.k.a. Buck. We still worked opposite shifts and opposite weekends so that we did not have to get a babysitter. Eventually, I went to first shift. We still worked in the same building but now different units. We had talked about moving in together, but the relationship had become somewhat strained. We finally parted ways.

Months had passed, and I did not contact him unless the baby was involved. We had made arrangements where he would keep our son on his weekends off, which meant that was my weekend to work. The arrangement worked fine. I was content without him. I was not one to chase a man down. I was not sitting home stewing. I was not ready to date again, but I went out once just to be doing something. I made it clear to the other person that I went out with no strings attached, no intimacy, no nothing, just going out to eat. The guy was a perfect gentleman and honored my request.

One day Russell showed up at my apartment. He told me that he wanted to make our relationship work. One thing that he was adamant about was that he did not want another man raising our son. We got back together. I laid down the law. He knew that I was once in an eight-year relationship with my high school sweetheart and that I did not marry my high school sweetheart. He had been in a ten-year relationship with his high school sweetheart, and they did not marry. I did not want to waste time with someone who could not commit long term in a relationship. With that said, I told him, "I will give you two years of my life. After two years, you should know by then if I am "the one" or if I ain't "the one." If I ain't "the one," then send me on my merry way because I will not give anyone that much time of my life without a commitment again." To this day, Russell cringes when we talk about this because he felt like I gave him an ultimatum. It was not that I gave him an ultimatum, I gave myself an ultimatum. I was going to make a choice after the two years were over.

The relationship continued to go smoothly. He gave up his apartment. We moved in together. He told me that if he ever proposed that there would not be a cloud in the sky. At that particular time, we had shared bank accounts. I noticed one day that a significant amount of money was missing. I didn't know how to approach him with it, so I gave him the benefit of the doubt. I said to myself, *Maybe this is the weekend that he will propose.* Not knowing if he would propose, I went ahead and got my nails done so that they would look pretty just in case he did propose.

That Saturday, we were on our way to Picadilles Cafeteria with our son. My daughter was with her dad. Russell said out of the blue, "My, there is not a cloud in the sky." I was beaming because I knew what it meant. Sure enough, while sitting at the table at Picadilles Cafeteria, he proposed. I was elated. I confessed that I was hoping that what he was doing since our bank account was missing some money. Otherwise, he would have had some explaining to do. For real.

We married on December 11, 1989. It was cold, and ice was on the road. One of my brothers and his fiancée at that time eloped with us. We went down to the wedding chapel in South Carolina. We were each other's witnesses. After we got our marriage license, we had to stay overnight to be married the following day. The night before the wedding, I was nervous, nauseous, had butterflies in my stomach, and had an upset stomach. I was a bundle of nerves because this was real. I had all the feelings that I did not have in my first marriage. I asked Russell if we were doing the right thing. He stated that he did not have any doubts. He assured me that this was what he wanted, to be a family. That eased my mind. The wedding went off the following day without a hitch. The four of us had so much fun and laughter. When we think about it now, we ask ourselves, *What in the world were we thinking about driving down to get married in the cold and icy weather?* I guess you can say that love makes you do crazy things.

Although Russell and I were married, he confessed years later that he was not ready to get married when we did. However, he knew that I was "the one" that he wanted to marry. He also stated that if he did not comply with my two-year rule, that he knew that I was going to walk away from the relationship. Rather than to lose me, he preferred to marry me instead. Not only that, but again, he did not want another man raising our son. He also raised my daughter, who is from my first marriage, since three years old. My daughter was blessed to have two dads who loved her. The two dads did not get along in the beginning, but as my daughter started her teens years, they became friends. Too friendly, I might add. We all had cookouts together. Then at some point, I told Russell that I did not want my ex-husband at all of our events. He agreed. However, the next cookout we had, who did I see coming up the driveway? Yep! My ex-husband. I left well enough alone. At least they were bonding. They became very close. When my ex-husband had a stroke, Russell was there to help him get up the stairs. It was beautiful to see the love for my daughter in both men. I teased Russell that he cried harder at my ex-husband's funeral than I did. He really did.

The main thing that made me knew he was the one was the way he treated my daughter. He made no difference between our son and my daughter. Whenever Russell introduced her to people, he always said, "This is my daughter." He never called her stepdaughter. As a matter of fact, he would say she looks just like him. Not! I knew marrying him was what I wanted to do. By the time he had come along in my life, I knew what I wanted in a relationship. I knew what I was going to tolerate in a relationship and what I was not going to tolerate in a relationship. I knew I deserved. I was not going to settle anymore.

Russell told me years later that he always said that he would never date a woman from a certain area, would never date a woman with a child, and would never date a woman who had been married before. Well, I had all three of these attributes. His explanation was that when he was a young boy, his family would come to the city to shop on Saturdays. He would see a lot of young pregnant girls. Therefore, he did not want to get involved with a girl from the city. Never say never!

My other confession: My husband does not know this yet. Not sure if I will tell him prior to release of this book. Here goes. I did not tell my husband before we got married that God was dealing with me. God was turning my life around. He was chastening me. I was at the point of where I no longer wanted to sin/shack up. I wanted to live right. My husband had left the wedding details up to me. I pushed up our wedding date because I knew God was doing something in my life. I thought that if I had told this to my husband before we got married that he might not wanted to go through with it. So I did not give him that option. Three months after we were married, I gave my life to Christ around March of 1990. The transition was hard, especially for my husband. The woman he had married was not the same woman he had dated. She changed. I changed. I went from being the confident, fun-loving, outgoing, extrovert girlfriend to being the submissive, introvert, religious wife. I did not know how to incorporate my newfound Christian walk into our marriage.

The change took a toll on our marriage in the beginning because I stopped everything cold turkey without warning. I stopped listening to love making music with my husband. I stopped slow dancing with my husband. I stopped wearing my "come get me" nighties. I started wearing frumpy gowns. It was hard putting the words "sexy" and "saint" in the same sentence. I did not feel comfortable being unclothed in front of my husband. I kind of knew how Eve in the Garden of Eden felt when she disobeyed God and hid from Him because she was naked and ashamed. I felt ashamed being naked before my husband. We had always had an active sex life. That dwindled also.

After getting saved, I no longer felt comfortable making love with my husband. I felt guilty and ashamed for enjoying such pleasure. I felt unclean in my mind. I felt like I was in bondage again. One day my husband approached me about our sex life. I knew that things had to change. I just did not know how to change it mentally so that I could change it physically. I eventually took baby steps back into the love making department. Some normalcy returned in the bedroom during that time.

During the transition, my husband had to make another adjustment. My attire had changed. I gave up wearing pants and just wore dresses. That was really hard for my husband to adapt. My husband hated it. I did not care to wear dresses daily either, but I went back to the traditions of the church. First our sex life went out the window, then here comes his wife with my dresses down to my ankles. I did not like mid-calf dresses. It was either knee-length or ankle-length. I chose ankle-length. It helped me to hide my body. I dressed that way for probably about a year.

A few things had changed my thought process, which made me started wearing pants again. One was that I wanted to go to Bible study one night. It was extremely cold. I really did not want to wear a dress. I told God that night that I really wanted to go to hear His Word. My choice was to not go and miss His Word or to be comfortable and wear pants and go hear His Word. I chose the latter. I felt that God knew my heart and that it was okay to go as I was. I wore my heart. I went to church with pants on. I am sure I got the stares, but no one even mentioned my pants.

The other thing that made me wear pants again and shortened the length of my dresses was something that my mother-in-law said to me. She said that because I wear my dresses to my ankles that my husband, her son, was not able to see my legs. She said that if he was not looking at my legs that he would be looking at some other woman's legs. That made sense. It got me to thinking. At some point, a group of us ladies from the holiness church were fellow-shipping. Apparently, we were talking about women's attire, particularly pants. Most likely, I brought up the subject since I was the one struggling with it. I remembered making the statement something to the fact that their husbands were saved. Their husbands were used to their wives wearing dresses and not showing their legs. Therefore, my husband was not saved. I felt that I had to dress somewhat more pleasing to my husband to maintain his attention.

After those revelations, I went back to wearing pants without wearing the guilt. My husband used to say to me, "I want my wife back," meaning the "old" me. Slowly a better version of the "old me" resurfaced. Apparently, we survived the transition. Here we are going on thirty-one years later of being married. I am now the confident, fun-loving, outgoing, extrovert, spiritual wife. After I got my mojo back, I started calling myself an "SS," a "sexy saint." Being sexy was not about the clothes I wore but more about my attitude and confidence about who I am as a woman in every aspect.

CHAPTER 7

Dreams and Demonic Spirits

When I first started having dreams that came true, I was in my mid-twenties. I lived in an apartment with my daughter who was a toddler. Russell and I were dating at that time. He lived in Creedmoor. On this particular day, we had spent the day together. It had snowed, and ice was on the road. We were on our way back home to my apartment from an outing. We were driving Russ' 1977 Oldsmobile. It was night time. Right in front of my apartment was a deep ditch before the entrance into the complex. A few feet before we reached the entrance, the car began to slide and spin out of control on the ice. We landed in the ditch. We were shaken up, but neither one of us were hurt. Immediately, it dawned on me that I had dreamed this prior to the accident. I thought this was just a coincidence, but now I know that God was dealing with me.

In 1989, Russell and I had built a home. Not sure how long we had been married before I started having dreams again. In 1990, I had accepted Christ Jesus as my Savior. Once I had accepted Him, I had a dream that I had made it over just in time. The dream was envisioned as a crack in the middle of the road. The road had shifted. One side of the road was higher than the other side of the road. Therefore, the other side was lower. I was standing on the lower side. A hand reached down to pull me upward. I believed the Lord had shown me that I had made it over just in time.

I had begun to dream about people whom I worked with that was going to die whom actually passed away after my dreams. The first three people that I dreamed had died were people whom I had contact with on the job. They were not really anyone whom I had a conversation with except to say "Good morning" or "Have a good evening." I really did not think anything of the dreams until the third person had died.

The third person had actually lived around the corner from me. She was my neighbor. After her death, I asked God if I was supposed to minister to these people. I continued to dream of people who was going to die. I knew that I had to go to them as I did not want their blood on my hands should they die without the opportunity to repent. After that, whenever I had dreams about people who were going to die, I would call each one and share that God wanted them to get their lives right and to repent. I did not tell them that I dreamed they had died. I did not want to frighten them but to shake them up to at least make a change in their lives.

This brings to mind the story in the Bible when Lazarus had died, and the rich man had died also. The rich man was in torment, and Lazarus was in the bosom of Abraham. The rich man wanted Lazarus to dip his finger in water and put on his (rich man) tongue to cool it as the fire was burning him. Abraham reminded the rich man of how he had lived and how Lazarus had lived. The rich man wanted Lazarus to go back from the dead and warn his five brothers of the torment that he was in and to warn them to repent so they would not end up in the place of torment where he was. Abraham told the rich man that his brothers have Moses and the prophets and that his brothers should listen to them. Besides if the brothers didn't listen to Moses and the prophets, they surely would not listen to someone from the dead (Luke 16:19–31). With that said, I felt that I did what God wanted me to do. I gave them the warning to repent. I do not know how many took heed to the warnings.

Have you ever been asleep but in the dream you are awake and can see everything in your home? This has happened often to me. This time it was associated with something darker. Mind you, any time I have had any of these encounters that my husband usually has exited the home, except on a couple of occasions.

While in this home, I had my first encounter with a presumed demonic spirit. One morning I was still in bed when my husband had left to go to work. I remembered laying on my stomach in bed and went back to sleep. I was startled and woke up. I was groaning and breathing heavily as if I had just had sex. I thought maybe it was with my husband, but I remembered that he had left for work. I got up and sat in bed trying to figure out what had just happened. A sexual encounter had occurred with someone or something. What I felt was real, but with what or whom?

On another occasion in that home, I had another encounter with a demonic spirit. One morning, my husband had left to go to work. I was still in bed laying on my stomach. While lying on my stomach, I had gone back to sleep. I felt something on my back. It appeared that I was awoke because I saw what was happening inside of my house. There was what appeared to be a "yellow hand" pressed into my back near my right shoulder. I reached around and grabbed the yellow hand and went into my kitchen. I turned on the stove and placed the yellow hand on the red-hot eye on the stove. The hand disintegrated and turned into ashes.

Again, here comes another encounter. My husband once again had left to go to work one morning. While lying in bed, this evil spirit came to me. By this time, I was beyond tired of dealing with the evil spirits. I remembered seeing the dark shadowy figure. I got out of my bed and walked toward the dark shadowy figure. As I walked toward the dark shadowy figure, it walked backward. I said to that demonic spirit, "I'm tired of you coming to me every time my husband leaves to go to work." I opened the kitchen backdoor as it continued to walk backward. I saw this dark shadowy figure go up the driveway and leave. After that, I did not have any more encounters with evil spirits in this house. Thank you, Lord.

In 1999, we had built another home and moved into it. We kept the first home as a rental property. Not long after, the dreams started happening again. This particular dream was, by far, the most surreal dream. In reality, my mom was living in our rental property. At that time, she and my sister were taking trips to Atlantic City. In my dream, I dreamed that the charter bus had put my mom off in front of our rental home where she was staying. In the dream, she was sick when she got off of the charter bus. In reality, that was the last time my mom went to Atlantic City.

One of my brothers had stopped by our mom's home to visit. He called me and stated that something was not right with our mom. I am a Registered

Nurse. He wanted me to assess the situation. When I arrived, our mom was coherent. She was not in pain. Her eyes were only able to shift to the left and forward, not to the right. We immediately took her to Duke Hospital in Durham, North Carolina. It was discovered that she was having seizures. After a brain scan, she was diagnosed with a brain tumor called Glioblastoma in 2006.

She had surgery to remove the tumor. The surgery was successful. However, we were told that this was a fast-growing tumor and that it usually would resurface in one year. She did not have to have IV chemotherapy, but she did have to take the chemotherapy pills. She did exceptionally well. She had put her trust in God to see her through this. Her life had returned to normal. She was able to live on her own. She had started driving again. We were able to breathe a sigh of relief. We gave God the glory and the praise because with Him, all things are possible. We stood on his Word and kept the faith.

Then one day, we received that dreadful call. Our mom's brain tumor had returned with a vengeance. This time the news hit my mom like a ton of bricks. Her enthusiasm and her hope had escaped her. It escaped us too. Still, we had to muster up some courage and continue to encourage our mom that it was going to be okay. This time our mom had to receive IV chemotherapy. It changed her life. It changed our lives. The chemotherapy made her weak. She could no longer live on her own. She moved in with me and my husband. I worked second shift at that time, so my husband looked after her while I was at work. My siblings and my dad would come over and help her with personal care. It did not dawn on me until years later that I should have taken family leave, but I was just so used to getting things done regardless.

Our mom lost her strength and had to go to a nursing facility for rehab only. That was the hardest subject to present to our mom. We did not want her to feel that we were putting her "away." She said to me, "Promise me that when I get better, I can come home."

I said, "I promise you will come home. This stay is only for rehabilitation so that you can get your strength back." Maybe a month after she was in the nursing facility, she had started having seizures. When I would visit her in the mornings before I went to work, I would observe the seizures and reported it to the nurse. Apparently, her condition was worsening. After a few months, the doctors stated that there was nothing else that they could do for our mom. This was on a Thursday.

I informed the doctors that I wanted to bring our mom home so that she could be with family. She came home with me that Thursday night. I had set up a baby monitor in her room so that I could hear her if she was in distress. The following day, Friday,

I was preparing to go to work. I had given our mom her bath and washed her hair that morning. Our dad was there in the room sitting with her. As I was ready to walk out of the door to go to work, I kissed our mom goodbye. I then noticed that her chest was not rising. I knew she was gone. I turned to our dad and let him know that she had passed away. My son was home. I gave him the bad news. We all wept.

Although we lost our mom in 2007, I found great consolation in the fact that she passed away in my home. I am so honored to have brought her home. I kept my promise. I believed she was waiting to "come home" just in time to "go home" with the Lord. My family had already released her so that she knew we were okay for her to enter into her eternal rest. She was so at peace through her sickness and transition. My other greatest consolation is that our mom was saved and had a relationship with the Lord. She and I had conversations about making sure she was right with God. She wanted to be sure. When we used to go to her appointments, we would sing Howard Hewett's song, "Say Amen." Sometimes now when I hear that song, tears roll down my face. I cherish those moments.

My dad and my mom had been separated since my senior year in high school. After the shock of the separation, they remained good friends. He lived in the country, and my mom had moved to the city. Ever since I could remember, my dad was and still is afraid of thunderstorms. He would come down town into the city to stay with my mom when storms occurred. He lived in the country and swore up and down that he would "never" live in the city. Around the corner from my mom's house was a blue single-family home. In my dream, my dad had moved down town into that blue single-family home around the corner from where my mom lived. I dreamed that my dad had died. I woke up in a panic and was crying because it seemed so real. I figured it was a just a bad dream because my dad swore he would never move to the city.

My husband calmed me in the middle of the night. I went back to sleep. I've never had this to happen before, but my dream picked up where it had left off. In my dream, I was back at the blue house where my dad was. He was laying in the casket with his funeral suit on. He said to me, "It's too late." Then I woke up crying again. It was a Sunday morning. I called my dad and siblings and requested that we gather together at my mom's house to tell them my dream. We all met there. I did not tell them who died in the dream. I told them that someone in our family had died and that God wanted us to get our life right. We hugged and told each other that we loved each other.

Lo and behold, not long after my dream, my dad actually moved to the city in that blue house around the corner from my mom's home. I was truly shocked because my dad did not like living in the city. I would have bet my paycheck that my dad would never ever move to the city. I knew then that my dream could possibly become a reality. Since I was the only one who knew that it was my dad who died in my dream, I knew that I had to go to him to make sure his life was right with God. It was one of the hardest things that I ever had to do: to talk to my dad about salvation. I had to go to that blue single-family home where he lived.

My dad and I had been close and had rekindled our relationship over the years, so I knew that we could have a conversation. We could talk about some things in my adult life. I needed to go to my dad. I mustered up the courage and went to visit my dad. After talking about other things with my dad, I ministered to him about salvation. I did not want to assume that he had accepted Christ. I needed to know that I know that he had accepted Christ in his life. He assured me that he had accepted Christ as his Savior. I believe we did the prayer of salvation anyway. I left that blue single-family home with joy in my heart knowing that my dad was saved. When my mom died and not my dad, according to my dream, I said to God that He did not show me that my mom was going to die, only my dad. Therefore, I was not prepared for my mom to die.

Another dream that I had was that our home was robbed. God had shown me in several dreams, approximately for over two years, that our home was going to get broken into. I told my husband about it several times. We did not prepare. Lo and behold, in 2006, our home was robbed. Right after that dream and robbery, I had a second dream that our home was broken into again. Sure enough, within ten days of the first robbery, our home was broken into again. You can best believe that we are well-equipped now for burglaries. Had we taken heed to the dreams, the warnings, the burglaries could have been prevented. Many times, a dream is not just a dream; it is a premonition or warning of things to come or things to prevent.

Years later, I began to deal with evil spirits again. The only time I had those encounters was when my husband had left to go to work or had exited the home, just like in our first home. Whenever my husband left for work, I would still be in bed because my work shift was later in the day. While still asleep on my side of the bed, I would feel a presence lay on my husband's side of the bed. I would actually feel the motion of the bed as if someone was there. I would be asleep, and I knew that it was not my husband.

In my sleep, I knew it was an evil spirit. Anytime I felt the presence of that evil spirit, I would call upon the name of Jesus. Once I say the name of Jesus, the evil spirit flees. There have been times when I could barely whisper the name Jesus due to restrictions from that evil spirit. However, just the whisper of Jesus's name had enough power to release me from the evil spirits. There is power in the Word of God.

> Submit yourselves therefore to God. Resist the devil and he will flee from you. (James 4:7 KJV)

I had gotten to a point where I told my husband to start waking me up before he left for work. That way, I could prepare myself for the unwanted evil spirits. So I dozed off to sleep after my husband got up for work one morning. After I fell back asleep, I felt the motion of someone or something on my husband's side of the bed. I felt the presence of that evil spirit. I began to call on the name of Jesus, and it went away. I woke up and said to myself, *I told my husband to wake me up before he left for work.* I got up and went up front toward the kitchen. I looked out the backdoor. My husband was outside in the yard. He had not left yet to go to work. I thought I was safe as long as my husband was around. I was wrong. However, I was safe because I was and am covered by the Blood of the Lamb. No demon in hell shall prevail against me.

One night in particular, my husband and I slept in another bedroom. Not sure why we did. That night while lying in bed with my husband, I apparently was lying on my stomach. Though I know I was asleep, there was a "hand" on my back trying to squeeze my lungs. There were these squeezing motions. My husband was lying beside me asleep. I was trying to call his name. My voice was straining because it felt like the air was being squeezed out of my lungs. I kept calling my husband's name. He could not hear me. I called on Jesus, and He heard me. When I spoke the name of Jesus, the hand disappeared. That was the only time that the evil spirit attacked me while my husband was in bed with me.

Another night, I had slept in that same bedroom alone. Either my husband was snoring loudly in our bedroom or maybe we were angry, I don't really remember. While asleep in the dark in the middle of the night, there appeared this mouth with no body attached to it. It was silver with jagged edge teeth. It was in my face chomping as to "shut me up." It wanted to take my words. I called upon the name of Jesus. It went away. Thank you, Jesus.

I called my pastors of the church. They came over a few days later. We all prayed. They had my husband to pray over me. I am not sure if I had to pray over my husband. They anointed our home. After the anointing of our home with prayer, I had no more encounters with those demonic spirits. Prior to our home being anointed and prayed over, I had started putting the Bible in bed with me after my husband went to work. I did it because this was the only way that evil spirit would not come near me.

Years had passed without any encounters with demonic spirits. By this time, I had purchased another home as my husband and I were on a break from marriage. My pastors came over to bless my new home. I knew I was good to go without demonic interferences. Then early one Saturday morning, here comes you-know-who. Right! Satan.

That night when I went to bed, I slept well up until about 4:00 a.m. Saturday morning when the encounter happened. I apparently was sleeping on my stomach. This evil spirit jumped on me and had me in a choke hold. I was struggling to call on the name of Jesus because of the choke hold. Once again, I was able to call on the name of Jesus. That evil spirit fled after calling on that powerful name of Jesus. After that encounter happened and I was free from that evil spirit, I got up and got ready for work. Of course, I thanked God for delivering me. I was still trying to figure out how that demonic spirit entered my home. I was baffled. *Why is this bad spirit in my home? My pastors had prayed over my home. How did this spirit enter my home?* I said to myself. I had to backtrack my thoughts to the day before, which was Friday.

I was home alone enjoying time to myself. I had rented a movie from this self-service video store. It was a relationship-type movie. As I was looking at the movie, it appeared different. I could not put my finger on it, but it appeared to be a very low-budget movie. Whenever I watch a movie and the scenes have bad language or inappropriate scenes, I would fast forward because I do not like those scenes; however, I liked the plot of the story. I am not sure if I finished the movie, but I don't believe that I finished because the vibes of the movie were really off. Then it came to my spirit that the evil spirit came from that movie. There were no telling what environment that movie had been. By now I was beyond angry with that evil spirit. How dare it invade my life again! I didn't have any anointing oil in that home. As soon as I got off of work, I went to Betty B's in Henderson to purchase some anointing oil. When I got home, I went to war. I anointed my home and rebuked those evil spirits. After that day, I was able to sleep peacefully. No more evil spirits. Needless to say, I never rented another movie from that place.

After that encounter, I knew that we have to be careful what we allow in our homes. This incident that I am ready to share will really blow your minds. By this time, I had been back in our marital home for three years since our break. Still no visits from evil spirits. Thank you, Lord. I will not say the name of this store, but I ordered three pairs of heels from this very expensive store. I had received two pairs and was waiting for the third pair. The third pair was black patent leather sexy heels. When the package arrived, I was excited.

After I opened the box, the excitement quickly faded. The pair that was sent to me was black. However, the heels were scuffed. Scratch marks were on the shoes. The name brand under the bottom of the shoe was completely worn off. I was truly disappointed with this product. Someone had worn this pair of shoes several times. I assumed that someone in customer service put their old worn shoes in the box and kept the new shoes. I called the shoe store and expressed my total disappointment and dissatisfaction. The customer service agent was apologetic and was going to send me the shoes that I had ordered. Meanwhile, I decided to wear this used pair of shoes to church on Sunday. Before I wore the shoes, I placed a cross and said a quick prayer over the shoes. Well, the story begins.

Day One: That Monday morning, the day after I wore *those* shoes, I went back to sleep after my husband had left for work. I apparently was in one of those dreams where I saw everything in my home. In that dream, I walked toward the front side of the house. I saw in the side ditch there was a large body of muddy water. In the front yard was a body of clear water. In my dreams whenever I see water, I would jump into the water as if I could swim. I cannot swim, but in my dreams I can swim. That is one of my goals. I did jump into the water and started swimming. On the other side of the house was grass. Now I am back in the house. I go back to bed so I can wake up. I tried to wake up but could not wake up. I lay back on my bed again in the same spot. I tried to wake up, but I could not wake up. I called on the name of Jesus and asked Him to wake me up. *Lord, please wake me up.* Then I woke up. Thank you, God.

Day Two: That morning, my husband had left for work once again. I entered into one of those dreams where I could see everything in my home. In that dream, I could see everything was dark inside of my home. It was dark outside as well. I did not understand the darkness. As I went towards the front of the house to the living room, a witch with a black hat on and a black garment on met me around the corner coming toward me. I began to plead the blood of Jesus. The witch disappeared. I went back to bed so that I could wake up. Again, I had to call on the Lord to wake me up. When I woke up, I was really baffled. Why are these evil spirits bothering me? I took my anointing oil and went to war in my home. I prayed, anointed my home, and rebuked those evil spirits.

Day Three: That morning after my husband had left for work, I entered again into another one of those dreams. This time in the dream, there were two little children bothering me while I was still in bed. I kept shooing them away so that I could go back to sleep and wake up. I remembered laying down a few times in the same spot so that I could wake up. I could not wake up. Again, I had to call on Jesus to deliver me. Okay, now I knew something was wrong. I was like, *Lord, why are these evil spirits in my home?* Then it was revealed. It was those shoes that I wore, those shoes that someone else had worn. Those shoes that someone had sent to me instead of the new shoes that I had ordered.

There were no telling what environment those shoes had been exposed to. I took those shoes, the box, and the bag that they came in and got them out of my home. I put them back in the mail to the department store. I didn't want anyone else to wear those shoes, but the department store was going to charge me for that pair if I did not return them. So I returned them. As a matter of fact, I returned all the shoes back to the department store.

I am not sure what the correct terminology for being asleep and yet awake in the dreams while seeing everything in your home. One thing I have discovered about this is that when I do experience the "can't wake up" episodes, it is because my body is tired and not ready to get up yet while my mind is saying get up you got things to do. It's like a battle of body versus the mind. Now those evil spirits that I experienced with those shoes are a totally different phenomenon. That definitely was about a demonic spirit.

I don't know why these evil spirits are so attracted to me. They don't bother my husband at all. My only consolation in this is that those evil spirits are trying to bind me to prevent me from carrying forth the assignment, which God has ordained for my life. The devil is a liar. I have victory over the enemy, even in my sleep. I thank God that the Blood still works. I am so thankful that I have enough Holy Spirit in me that I can call on the name of Jesus in my sleep, and He delivers me from the hand of the enemy.

> For I know the plans I have
> for you, declares the Lord, plans
> to prosper you and not harm you,
> to give you hope and a future.
> (Jeremiah 29:11 NIV)

Thank God that I have not experienced any more of those demonic episodes to date.

Not all of my dreams have had evil connotations. I have had some beautiful dreams. When my daughter was pregnant with her first two children, I had dreamed it beforehand. She did not approach me with the information. I approached her. She confirmed that I was right. I did not dream about the third pregnancy. Now all of them are teenagers. My son has one teenager and one toddler. I have a total of nine grandchildren. I know my daughter's three children and my son's two children do not add up to nine. Some of them have other siblings and cousins who call me and my husband their grandparents, so we claim them all. You should see my mantle above the fireplace at Christmas with all of their names on their stockings. It's a beautiful sight being able to witness a legacy of love and to be able to count my many mini blessings.

Okay, back to the dreams. I had one of the most beautiful visitations from the Lord I will always remember. In this dream, there was a round bright glow floating toward me. It had the biggest smile on its face. It was like a Kool-Aid smile. It was right in my face. I heard the voice say, "Tell my people in both ears that what I promised them in secret will come to pass." Then it kissed me on my left cheek and went away. I knew that it was from God. I know how it feels now when someone shakes hands or touches a celebrity and they don't want to wash their hands because of that special moment. That is how I felt. I really did not want to wash my left cheek for I felt that I had been kissed by the Lord.

CHAPTER 8

Mental Illness

"Mental illnesses are health conditions involving changes in emotion, thinking or behavior (or a combination of these). Mental illnesses are associated with distress and/or problems functioning in social, work or family activities. Mental illnesses are common (American Psychiatric Association). According to the APA, "Nearly one in five US. adults experience some form of mental illness."

Mental illness, also called mental disorder, is real. Many of us know someone who is battling this disease even in our own families. As you can see, it runs in my family, even in myself. I deal with mental health issues as well. These issues may not be as severe compared to what I have seen other people go through. For me, there would be a battle going on in my mind that would plague me. My thoughts would hold me captive sometimes, making me a prisoner in my mind. The battle is not usually evident on the outside. If it is evident, it is minimal in my perspective. What I now realize is that I was battling mental illness in my youth as well. I do believe some of these behaviors stem from traumas from my childhood/adulthood. I also know some of it is inherited. According to research released, mental disorders can be the results of both genetic and environmental factors. I can attest to this because few of my family members share the same disorder called Skin Picking or Dermatillomania.

It is a mental illness disorder related to obsessive-compulsive disorder. I struggle with the disorder. My skin has to be smooth, especially around my fingernails. I cannot have a hang nail or jagged cuticles. I will pick at it until it is smooth. I will obsess in removing the unwanted or unnerving skin. Sometimes, I would end up with all fingers bleeding or sore. One time, I had band-aids on all ten fingers because I picked until they bled. I know it is gonna hurt, but I do it anyway. The area has to be smooth. Even when I get a manicure at the nail shop, my polish is perfect. However, if one fingernail polish chips, then I will pick at the rest of the nails until all the polish is off. They have to be uniformed.

I did not know this until before my mother passed away that she too was a skin picker. I think my case was worse as I never saw her hands damaged. Another family member admitted to picking at their fingers as well. I see compulsive tendencies in my daughter also. Let's just say you won't find any dust in her house. Okay, she's obsessive with cleaning. She constantly wipes down things even on her job. She says that it's a comfort for her. Shaking my head for my grandkids.

By working in the medical field, I have seen others with this condition. I have never been diagnosed because I have never presented this information to any medical professional. A hair out of place or a wrinkle in my clothes do not bother me. It's just compulsive actions with my fingers. My husband tells me sometimes, "I know your fingers get tired of you." He says that because sometimes while watching a movie, I am constantly picking at my hands. Maybe because I am not busy or not moving. Many times, it is due to anxiety. He sometimes would hold my hands together so that I would not pick. Sometimes it works. Sometimes it doesn't. He says that I am going to peel myself like a banana one day. My husband has a lot of quirky sayings that no one else would come up with. Let's just say he gets it honestly.

I have had other obsessive-compulsive thoughts. I used to be extremely hard on myself. Actually, I still am at times, but I am a lot better in allowing myself to make mistakes and not punishing myself for it. In my childhood, I went through a stage of perfectionism. That "one thing" had to be right or perfect. For example, when I was a child, if I wrote on a piece of paper, it had to be perfect. There could not be any marks on it, not even eraser marks. If I made a mistake, I would continue to ball up paper and throw it away until I had a perfect paper. By the time I would finish, the floor would be covered with balled up papers.

When my daughter first started school, I saw her do the same thing when she wrote in her journal. She was aiming for perfection. I saw myself in her. I realized then that she could end up like me obsessing over something minor. Right then, I let her know that it was okay to make a mistake. That paper did not have to be perfect. One of the things I helped her do was to create a draft. That way, she could make mistakes and form her thoughts before completing the final document. This paid off. She was an excellent student, even president of the National Honor Society in middle school. After that day, I did not see her trying to be perfect. As a matter of fact, one day she had painted her fingernails red. I happened to be in the shower. I heard her screaming and crying. I ran out of the bathroom. Red polish was all over hands like she was bleeding. She thought she was bleeding. I was relieved that it was not blood. I was also relieved that she was not crying because her fingernail polish was not perfect.

In my pre-teen years, I remembered occasions when I began to obsess over thoughts. One occasion was when we lived in the country. The last house that we lived in as a family was a two-story house. We would be upstairs playing. As kids, we used to pretend that we were going into town. We would slip into our sleeping bags and slide in our sleeping bags down the stairs. The sleeping bags were slick and shiny, so it was easy to get a fast ride "into town." One day while upstairs, my mom called me to come downstairs. I said, "I will be down." Then I thought, *Did she thought I cuss?* Did she think I said, "I will be damn?" It bothered me that she might thought I had cussed her. I had internalized that over and over and over in my head. That thought caused me so much anxiety and stress as a child.

I also remembered over obsessing over a matter in my senior year of high school. I was preparing to take senior portraits with the drape on. That night before picture day, I had rolled up my hair to have curls for my picture. The next morning, all of my curls had fallen out by the time I got to school. I took the picture anyway. When the picture draft came back, I did not like my portrait. It was not perfect. I did not want anyone to see my portrait. I was trying to find a way to not have my portrait shown in the yearbook. It drew me crazy.

My thoughts were crazy. I thought, *How could I get rid of those yearbooks?* The thought came to my mind was to burn down the school. That was the only way that I could accomplish making those yearbooks go away. That thought played in my head over and over and over again. How could I do it and get away with it? I was obsessed with that thought. It consumed me. It overwhelmed me. I think what made that thought go away was that it was time to take cap and gown portraits. I was going to redeem myself. I took the cap and gown portrait. I liked that portrait better. I felt relieved. I stopped obsessing. No one knew how dangerously close in my mind I had come to committing a crime due to not being able to control a thought.

Not only was I obsessing over my hair, I was obsessing over my smile. I had a defect, which I was trying to hide. In my senior year of high school before senior pictures, my face was paralyzed. I did not realize it until one of my friends pointed it out at the lunch table. What happened was that me and another guy were walking out of the cafeteria. We had to go through double steel doors. When the door swung back, I did not catch it. It hit me smack in the face. I did not feel the pain. I only felt the jolt of the door.

So the next day was when my friend discovered there was something wrong with my face. She said that one side of my face was not moving, that my left eye was not blinking, and that I was not smiling on that side. I thought she was playing until she said that she was serious. I got up from the lunch table and went to the bathroom. Sure enough, I could not smile or blink my eye on the left side of my face. I called my parents. They took me to Duke Hospital. I remembered the doctors sticking pins in my face to see if I felt it. I did not feel it. They said that I had something like Bell's palsy, a type of facial paralysis. I do not remember the actual name for it. The doctors felt confident that the sensation would return to my face.

I do not remember how long it took for the sensation to return to my face, but I was still in my senior year of high school. I think it was maybe a few months. Thank God, but I had some residual effects from the incident. The jolt apparently shifted the left side of my face to a slight degree. When I blink, even to this day, the right side of my mouth twitches. If I slightly move the right side of my face toward the left side, I can see where it should be better aligned. My sister apparently had forgotten about the trauma with my face. She had moved away for a few years. When she returned and saw me, she asked if I had a stroke. I said that I did not have a stroke. I reminded her of the incident at school that had affected me, particularly my mouth.

At times, I can see how someone thought I may have had a stroke. Whenever I take pictures, I try to remember to shift my mouth toward the left a little so that the alignment of my face would be symmetric. I also have to remember to either squint one of my eyes or open them wide in order to look symmetrical in photos due to the facial injuries. I am super self-conscious about taking pictures because sometimes I do forget to shift my mouth. If my mouth looks twisted in a photo, I am very hard on myself about it. If the picture is still in someone's camera, I would ask them to retake the pictures over and over and over again until I like the photo. They do not know why I keep asking for retakes. Sometimes I try to avoid taking pictures.

While writing this topic, I asked my husband about mental illness. Did he see any signs of mental illness in me? He replied, "Yes."

He recalled when my five-year-old daughter was preparing for her first year of school. I do not know how we got on this subject, but I had said something about sending her to school with a knife in kindergarten. I don't know why I made that statement. Apparently, it was for her to protect herself. I don't know why I felt that she would need protection in school at that age. He thought that was the craziest thing to say. I totally agreed. That was not a stable statement. And no, I did not send my daughter to school with any weapons. I never thought about it again. However, I am ashamed to confess that I had a thought of fatally harming my children when they were small. I did not want them to experience the pain that I had experienced in this cruel world. I knew that they would automatically go to heaven. But I loved them too much to cause them pain. So I vowed to love them unconditionally and protect them with every fiber of my being, as well as to raise them in the church. They both have beautiful families of their own to love and protect. Thank you, God, for guarding my heart and my mind. I did not share that statement with my husband or anyone. That thought was definitely a sign of mental instability/illness.

Like my deceased brother, I have a daily mantra. It is "Thank you, Lord." I constantly tell Him *thank you* several times throughout the day because I am so, so grateful that He picked me up out of the mud and mire clay and placed my feet on the solid rock to stand. I remembered driving down the road one day with my son who was a teenage at that time. I blurted out loud, "Thank you, God."

My son answered, "You're welcome," as if he was God. We both fell out laughing. It is just a habit of mine to give God thanks regardless of where I am and apparently regardless of who I am with.

Have I ever sought help for any of my traumatic experiences? Not really. Okay, no. There was a family physician when I was in my early twenties who knew about some of my childhood issues but not all of my issues. If I had a voice back then and shared my traumatic experiences with the doctor, I believe that he would have been obligated to report the sexual assault and probably had me committed for evaluation for suicidal thoughts/attempts. He had suggested that maybe I needed to see someone in the mental health department. I said I would although I did not. I did not want to be labeled at a young age. However, I am not against treatment if I needed it.

I have been treated for anxiety, panic attacks, and depression. I could not tolerate those medications because of the side effects. I understood when my deceased brother was on medication and how it made him zombie-like, walking and talking in slow motion. One medication that I had received when dealing with anxiety made me feel the same way. The effects that it had on me were intolerable. I would arrive to my destination and did not remember how I got there. I remembered going to the mall with my family. We ran into another family there. It was as if that family had appeared out of nowhere. I realized that this medication had made me feel "out of it." I was definitely not myself. I remembered falling asleep on the job. No matter how tired I was or how sleepy I was, I never slept on the job. This medication was affecting my overall being. I stopped taking the medication. I returned back to my normal self, whatever that was.

CHAPTER 9

The Power of Words

Depression had plagued me from childhood into adulthood. One of the reasons for the depression was that I did not have a voice. I was an introvert. I did not stand up for myself. I did not know how to stand up for myself. I was invisible. I did not know how to say no. I let people run over me. I was tired of surviving. I wanted to thrive.

In my early twenties, I had started taking antidepressants on and off. I realized that once the medication wore off, I was still depressed. I went back to my family doctor and told him, "I don't want to be on antidepressant pills the rest of my life."

He said to me, "Well, this is what you need to do. I want you to know that you matter. I want you to put yourself first because you are *somebody.*" When he said those words, I became alive. The dark clouds went away in my life. Someone believed in me. Someone said the words that I had longed to hear that *I matter.* I kind of felt like Rudolph the Red-Nosed Reindeer. Rudolph was down on himself because his nose was red. He was different from the other reindeers. He felt like he was a misfit. I could relate. Then he met the female reindeer, Clarice. She gave him life changing words. Rudolph said, "She said I'm cute! I'm cute!" Rudolph's confidence was built up. He started holding his head up. He was ready for the challenge ahead of him.

After that day, just like Rudolph, I was on a mission to rescue me. I was no longer the "Yes" girl. I told people, "No" when I felt like it, and it felt good. I started doing things that I wanted to do. I no longer did what people expected of me. I no longer allowed people to talk to me in any manner. As a matter of fact, that is my main peeve today: how a person speaks to me. I always try to respect people. But I also command and demand respect as well. After my newfound appreciation for myself, I constantly stayed in the director's office at work. I had found my voice. I was using my voice. I was telling people off. I was in their faces. I went from being timid to being aggressive. I did not have a middle ground.

I remembered once during an interview around that same time, the interviewer asked me, "Why should I hire you?"

I told her, "Because I thought enough to apply for the job." That was a cocky and aggressive answer. That's how sure I was of myself, maybe too sure.

My husband, whom I was dating at that time, told me, "You just can't tell folks off every time they say something that you don't like." I thought about it. I agreed. I knew that I had to find a middle ground. I became assertive. I no longer was called into the director' office for telling off folks. I was still able to tell people what I wanted them to know with respect and calmness. It took me a while to get there, but I got there. I gained my confidence. I knew who I was. I was/am *somebody*. For the first time, I loved me. I had found myself.

A year later, I had another interview with the same person whom I gave that cocky answer to. She told me that she saw a world of difference in me compared to the first interview. My attitude was less cocky. Needless to say, I did not get either job. It was okay for I had gained something far better: my voice.

I did not always recognize depression. Usually I could tell when depression was setting in. Other times, it just snuck up on me. To ward off depression, back in the day, I slept a lot to avoid thinking. Today, prayer is the number one key. I pray to overcome depression. When depression tries to set in now, it seems like the enemy wants to take my voice, to take my words. When I try to pray when depression sets in, my voice is so low that I could barely hear it. I keep praying. My voice gets loud. I keep praying. My voice gets louder. My voice becomes so loud that it drowns out the enemy's voice. I take back my power. I have the authority to put the enemy under my feet. He will not conquer me.

> Greater is He that is in me than
> he that is in the world. (1 John 4:4
> KJV)

He is a defeated foe. To also help ward off depression, I acknowledge what "that thing" is that is making me depressed. I speak my truth. I then try to eliminate "that thing" from my life. The lesson I learned regarding depression and other matters of life is that if you do not control "that thing," "that thing" will control you. I know now that I have the power to make that change. I have the Word of God in me and the Holy Spirit who lives in me to guide me into all truth. As Glinda the Good Witch said to Dorothy in the *Wizard of Oz*, "You've always had the power, my dear. You've had it all along." That is one of my favorite movies.

I knew about God growing up, but I did not know His love for me. I discovered His unconditional love when I started attending Cornerstone Christian Community Church where I am still a member. I remembered when I first started going how much love I felt from the people. The messages were so uplifting, so encouraging. The presence of God was there. I felt free, though I had not been healed yet. I was still suffering in silence. After everything that I had been through, I was a broken soul. I felt like Humpty Dumpty. I could not imagine being put back together again. Each Sunday that I went, I wept and I wept. I was in so much mental and spiritual pain. I needed healing. I needed new breath, new life. I needed a touch from the Master's hand.

Going to this church was the first time that I realized how much God loved me—a depressed, unworthy individual. He really loved me. In spite of my faults, he still loved me. I realized that He loved me more than He wanted to send me to hell. God did not want me to go to hell. His only begotten Son died for me so that I would live and live an abundant life. He knew that I needed saving. He knew that I needed deliverance. He knew that I needed restoration.

No matter how broken I was, I kept going to this new church. I kept crying. I kept praying. I kept going to the altar for prayer. I did not stop. I wanted to stop. I could not stop. I didn't want to go up in front of the church sobbing. I was desperate. My heart was heavy. I did not want to leave the church the same way that I came into the church: bounded. I kept pressing my way to the altar, still weeping. I felt like the woman who had the issue of blood for twelve years.

With her issue, she was not supposed to go out in public, let alone touch someone. She made her way through the crowd. She knew that Jesus was the only One who could heal her. She needed the Physician. She reached down and touched the hem of His garment. When she touched Jesus's hem, the Bible says that the power had gone out from Him. Jesus asked, "Who touched me?" The woman came trembling and fell at the feet of Jesus and said that it was her who touched Him. Jesus saw her faith. He said to her, "Daughter, your faith has healed you. Go in peace and be freed from your suffering" (Luke 8:43–48 KJV).

Believing in Jesus Christ was the only One who could take away my pain. He was my only Hope. I knew that if He could heal that woman, he could heal me. There were times when I literally reached out and pretended to touch Jesus's garment. That was how desperate I was. I needed to be made whole.

Today, I am no longer depressed, oppressed, or suppressed. I can say with total confidence that Jesus touched me. He saw my faith. He made me whole. He healed me of past hurts. He casted my sins and pain into the sea of forgetfulness. He wrapped His loving arms around me. There were times when I needed the pain to go away so badly that I would ask Jesus to literally wrap His arms around me. I needed to feel His presence. He held me. His righteous right hand upheld me. He never let go of me. He never forsook me. That is why I love Him so much. That is why I bow in His presence. That is why I still cry tears of joy. He cared enough to not only receive my prayers but to answer my prayers.

I began to read His Word. I took Him at His Word. His Word shaped my life. To think that I was created in His image was profound. To think that He gave His only begotten Son to die for me, an unworthy sinner. To think that I am fearfully and wonderfully made. To think that I am the apple of His eye. To think that God chose me. He hand-picked me. I used to say that I chose Him, but after reading His Word, I feel honored that He chose me. His Word says that He chastens those whom He loves. He chastened me so that meant He loved me. He drew me. His Word says that if we draw closer to Him, He will draw closer to us. He dragged me back to Him. I cultivated my relationship with Him. All these things that I had encountered was not for naught. God had a purpose for me even through my pain. That is how this book was birthed: from my pain. I am a living witness that dry bones can live.

One thing that I have learned is that when we take the focus off of ourselves, we can see God in our situation. With that said, I began to plug into areas in the church. I began to usher. I joined the hospitality committee. I joined the Rest Home Ministry team. Each member of the team was given the opportunity to bring forth a message for the clients and staff. I am an intercessor. I am currently a student in Northeastern Regional Bible College. I joined the Hand-n-Hand Dance and Drama Ministry. I loved being on the drama team. I had the opportunity to play someone that I am not. Usually I played the bad guy.

In real life, I try to be the good guy, so whenever I got the chance to be bad, I enjoyed being bad. I remember one year I believe it was our Easter play. I played one of the bad characters who wanted Jesus crucified. I kept yelling, "Kill Him! Kill Him! Nail Him to the cross!"

After the play, the children who were in the play came up to me and said, "You are mean! You wanted to kill Jesus!"

I said, "Sweetie, I am just playing the bad guy. I love Jesus just like you do." I thought that was so sweet that they wanted to take up for Jesus. When I think about it, Jesus took up for me. He sacrificed His life for me. He hung, bled, and died for me. I thank God for His Word that says, "There is therefore now no condemnation to those who are in Christ, who do not walk according to the flesh, but according to the Spirit" (Romans 8:1 NKJV). I no longer walk in condemnation. I no longer walk in defeat. I no longer beat myself up for what happened or what did not happen. I walk in victory. I still encourage myself. I know who I am: a child of the Most High God. I am not saying that I do not have struggles. Trust me, I still have struggles.

I am not one who seeks recognition, but sometimes it comes along with the journey. I have to admit that it took great courage to step out on faith. I was super afraid to step out. While taking a course in Northeastern Regional Bible College, we were studying the Book of Acts. We were talking about how some of the apostles and disciples most likely were afraid on their journey. My instructor said, "Do it even if you have to do it scared." I thanked her. It was confirmation for me in dealing with my fears to come up higher and have the courage step into the things that God is calling me into for His glory. She did not know my journey nor that I am writing this book. Now I am doing it, scared but excited also. I do not want to hide any longer. I want to own it: my identity, my calling, my purpose. At the end of the day, it is not about me but about what God wants to accomplish through me.

> What you say can preserve your life or destroy it; so you must accept the consequences of your words. (Proverbs 18:21 GNT)

This scripture is self-explanatory. Our words have power. I am a witness. My son had two babies that had passed away. One baby died at four months old from crib death. The other baby died at five months old in her mother's womb. It was a stillbirth. I shared some, if not more, of the guilt of my grandbabies' death. Prior, I had made a comment to my children. "Y'all need to stop having these babies." Although they were not married, I was going to love and support them anyway. That is just my nature.

However, I still made the comment. I don't think it dawned on me until the loss of the second baby that I remembered those dreadful words that I had spoken. My heart grieved. I spoke death, not life. I had to go to my son. I repented to God. I repented to my son. I felt responsible. Now my son has a beautiful toddler, my granddaughter named Shiyonna. I am so grateful for her. She brings so much joy in our lives. My son is in love with his baby girl. He hardly ever lets her out of his sight. He dotes on his baby girl. I don't blame him. Sometimes I tell him he is too obsessed over her. After losing two children, he has that right to shower her with all his love. You can bet from now on that I choose my words rightly. What you say will either bless you or curse you. Be blessed and choose life words.

There is something magical and mystical about speaking words into the atmosphere, not just thinking words. Abraham did not have any children at this time, but God said that Abraham would be the father of many nations. Abraham believed God. He was counted as righteousness with God. Abraham had faith. His promise depended on his faith. Faith is believing what we cannot see. Romans 4:17 (AMP) says to speak of the nonexistent things as if they existed.

To speak, we have to open our mouths and allow words to form. God did not say to think. He said to "speak." Words take flight, and they come back in full circle. When I am talking to God, many times I speak to Him outwardly. I make sure He hears me believing that what I speak will come to fruition.

Isaiah 55:11 (NIV) says:

> So is my word that goes out from my mouth: It will not return to me empty, but will accomplish what I desire and achieve the purpose for which I sent it.

God's Words have power. The Holy Spirit lives in us. Therefore, we have power. We need to exercise the power that is within us.

The Holy Spirit just reminded me of something that I said in the interview where I gave that cocky answer. The interviewer asked me what I saw myself doing in five years. I said, "I wanted to write a book." I actually said it to impress the interviewer. That was in the mid-1980s. As my husband and I were talking about this section of my book, he shared also how I used to say that I wanted to be an author. Oh my goodness. Who would have thought it? Again, words have wings and will come back in full circle. I am a living witness.

CHAPTER 10

A Shifting Taking Place

Have you ever been dismissed from a job and was glad about it? I have. I was working at a clinic. I was supervisor over three nurses. I did not want to be supervisor. I was retired and did not want the responsibility. I did not want to deal with attitudes. I wanted do my job and go home. It was a good job with good perks. I enjoyed going to work at that time. The only downfall was that I had to get up at 4:00 a.m. to get ready for work. What was I thinking? Evidently, it was not by coincidence that I was there. There was a person there whom I was ministering to. At some point, this person was no longer working at the job.

About the next month after that person was gone, things began to change for me. I was not able to sleep at night. I would wake up the same time almost nightly. Many times I got up to pray. I was questioning God what is it? Why could I not sleep at night? Someone on the job suggested sleeping pills. I refused to take sleeping pills. I stated that I would find another job before taking medication to help me sleep. Each morning before going to work, I felt fine. Shortly after arriving to work, I would feel yucky. My eyes would hurt and burn. My blood pressure would be elevated. I just did not feel good at work. I only felt like this at work. I did not have any of these symptoms when I was home.

I had gotten to the point where I hated going to work. Again, it had good perks. Practically every day I would say to myself, *Stay or quit? Stay or quit?* I talked myself into staying. I would put a fake smile on my face, but on the inside, I was miserable. On my morning breaks, I would walk around the building admiring God's beauty, His creations. I would say to myself, *Lord, I would love to be home sitting on my front porch right about now.* I said it often.

One week after coming from vacation, I noticed that the atmosphere at work had changed. I was not sure why. People were kind of like in hiding. Around lunch time, my boss told me that he wanted to see me after lunch. I said, "Okay." I asked the Holy Spirit, *Why does my boss want to see me?*

The Holy Spirit said, *This is your last day here.*

I said to the Holy Spirit, *But why? What have I done?* Then I said, *You know what, it doesn't matter why. If the Holy Spirit said this is my last day, then this is my last day.* I had my answer. Sure enough when

I went into the boss' office, he informed me that it was my last day there.

I said to him, "When your season is up, your season is up." He thought I would be upset and offered to talk over the weekend or meet over the weekend. I declined and told him I was good. He did not know that he had just did me a favor. I thanked him and gathered my belongings. I remembered too that very morning that I said to God while on break, *I would love to be home sitting on my front porch.* God made it happened.

The following day, I truly enjoyed sitting on my front porch. I was actually enjoying being retired. I told God, *Lord, I am enjoying sitting on my front porch. You should have let my boss fire me a long time ago.* I sent my boss an email to thank him. I thanked him for having the courage to do what I did not have the courage to do. He made the choice so that I did not have to. I told him that it was in God's plan; therefore, I could not be mad at what God was doing. I knew my season was up. I just did not exactly know why at that time.

About one and a half years later, it was revealed why my season was up. I was there to minister to that individual who had left the job. My work was done. My assignment was completed. It was time for me to move on. It took me too long to move, so God intervened. After leaving that job, I no longer had any ill symptoms. I felt relieved. I felt free. Thank you, Lord.

Two months later, I was hired back at the job from whence I had retired to work part-time. Let me share how God showed up. When I was offered the job, it was for early morning hours. I knew right off the bat that I could no longer work early hours. Been there, done that, didn't want to do it again. Getting up at 4:00 a.m. at my last job had a negative effect on me. With that said, I swore off early morning hours. One thing about working at this particular workplace is that when you retire, you can pretty much set your own hours. Here I was stressing over the early hours that was offered. I contacted the nursing department to let them know that I could not work those hours and asked if I could go in a little later to work. It was stated that these are what the hours were for this job. I said, "Okay," but I had not accepted the job. I went into prayer mode.

I said to God, *Okay, God. You know that I can't work those early hours, so I need You to do something. I need You to move on my behalf. If this is the job for me, then let them work with my hours. If not, then I am good staying home retired.* After my prayer, I was at so much peace. I was resolved that if the nursing department did not agree to work with my hours, then I was going to decline the job offer and be absolutely okay with my decision. About an hour and a half later, I received a call from the nursing department. I was offered a job with mid-morning hours instead of early hours. Yay! Won't He do it? What I learned is that stressing does not move God. Trusting and resting in Him does.

Starting off the job was fine. I enjoyed working there. About four to six months into the job, I started having the same symptoms as at the other job. I felt fine before going to work. Once I got to work, I felt horrible. My eyes hurt and burned. My blood pressure was elevated. I recognized the signs this time. I knew my season was coming to an end at that job even though I had only been there for a few months when I recognized what was happening. It was difficult to leave the job right away because one of the nurses was on maternity leave and another nurse was in nursing school. That left our department short of nurses. I did not want to make matters worse for the department. I hung in there a little while longer until I became ill and had to take time off to recuperate.

At some point, I got really sick. At first, I thought that it was due to a new medication that I was taking for issues with reflux. Whatever it was, God had my attention. I felt to the point of death. My body and my mind were tired and felt like giving up. Praise God that the Holy Spirit did not agree with what my mind and my body were telling me. I did not share with anyone, not even my husband, how close to death I felt until later. This was between me and God. I had to cry out to God literally. I needed heaven to touch earth on my behalf. I understood when the writer said that the grave cannot praise You, but the living shall praise You. It felt like I was fading out of this world. I told God that I did not want to leave this world because I had not done what He had called me to do. I knew He was calling me up higher. I had to accept my assignment.

I thought my walk with God was better than okay. I come to realize that I could not serve God with a mediocre spirit. I had to be all in. I thought I was all in. The scripture came to mind about the ten virgins—five wise virgins with oil in their lamps and five foolish virgin with little oil in their lamps. I felt like one of the foolish virgins. It felt like the oil in my lamp was low. In fact, to be honest about it, it felt like my oil was depleted. I needed some oil. I needed new oil. I asked God to refresh me. I started going back to Bible Study. I did not think that Bible Study was that important since I plugged into other areas spiritually. Oh, how wrong I was.

Bible Study was one of the stations where I had to go to fuel up on the Word of God. I also plugged into Sunday School to fuel up as well. I no longer wanted to take God for granted. I no longer wanted to take God's Word for granted for He is the Word. God heard my cry. Once I started filling up at these spiritual filling stations, I immediately felt rejuvenated. I felt revived. I felt alive. I felt renewed. I felt resurrected. I felt the move of the Holy Spirit in my life. God had to take me down to the lowest point, even to the brink of death, to grasp hold of the purpose He has planned for my life. What I went through was not to destroy me but to elevate me.

After I recovered and went back to work, I knew beyond the shadow of a doubt, what I had to do. I knew that I had to resign from that job. My supervisor was a Christian. I shared with her the revelation behind the symptoms that I was experiencing. I shared that my season was up and that it was time for me to leave. She understood. She told me she knew that my season was up. She said that I had come there to do what I was supposed to do, which was "to minister" to her. It was bittersweet leaving. God had moved me once off of a job. I was not going to be disobedient this time. I heard Him this time in my spirit. I resigned. No regrets. Once I resigned, I no longer had those ill symptoms again. Do the math! It's like that old saying, "You don't have to eat the whole cow to know that you are eating beef." In other words, I don't have to lose another job or my life to know that God is shifting things in my life for His purpose.

Two months had passed. I am always talking to God. I shared with Him that I desired extra funds to be able to bless His people. I found a job working only one day a week. About two months into the job, COVID-19 surfaced in the land.

Our facility was shut down even though we were COVID-free. I eventually went home to enjoy retirement finally. I really, really enjoyed my retirement. Apparently, one of the assignments was for me to write my book. Had it not been for the pandemic that surfaced, I would not have taken the time to write my book. I had a thought in the back of my mind for years to write a book, but that was all it—a thought, which now has come to fruition. I knew that this was my season to make my mark in 2020–2021.

What I know about seasons is that seasons change. When you stay in a season too long, things become stagnant. Things begin to wither and die. I thought about what if it was summer all year round. The heat would kill the grass. Vegetation would dry up. Mankind would perish. That is how I felt staying too long in a season. I was drying up like I was dying. After getting dismissed from one job, sick to the point of near death on another job, and the last job shut down, it is clear that God is shifting things in my life.

CHAPTER 11

The Favor of God

Favor is an act of kindness beyond what is due or usual. Favor of God is divine kindness. The Lord is in accord with the individual and has shown gracious kindness toward them (Compelling Truth). So shall you find favor, good understanding, and high esteem in the sight of God and man (Proverbs 3:4 Amplified Bible).

One of my favorite songs is "God Favors Me" by Hezekiah Walker. I even had a sign on the front of one of my vehicles that said God Favors Darlene. I made it personal because He knows my name. "He knows My Name" is another one of my favorite songs by Tasha Cobbs Leonard. When I was at my former church, there was a family whom I envied when I was a child because I saw the favor of God on them. I was young and did not know about favor, but I knew that they had something special from God. I remembered saying to myself and God's ears that I wanted that kind of favor. I also remembered saying that if Christ came that I wanted to ride the matriarch's coattail of that family to heaven because she was definitely anointed by God. As I grew in the knowledge and saving grace of my Lord and Savior, I come to realize that this was an individual walk. I had to work out my own soul and salvation. I will have to stand before God for myself. Therefore, I had to seek Him and form a personal relationship with my Creator.

As I began to serve in His kingdom, I began to experience His favor. I began to see special things happening in my own life, in my family. Yay! I have the favor of God. I did not just seek His hand, I sought His face, His grace, His favor. One of my favorite sayings I say to those who needs a special blessing from God is that, "If you seek the face of God, He will definitely show you His hands." In other words, the blessings will come down when the praises go up.

> But seek ye first the kingdom
> of God and His righteousness and
> all these things shall be added to
> you. (Matthew 6:33 NKJV)

Though I was not attending church at that time, God's hands were always covering me. His angels were encamped around me. There was a time when Russell and I were dating and had just gotten back into town from vacation. I had decided to run some errands alone. I was driving on Lewis Street by Burlington Mills Plant. I happened to look in my rearview mirror. This car was speeding so fast. I knew it was going to hit me. I was praying to not let the car hit me and braced myself. As the car came upon me, it put on screeching brakes and fishtailed at the very last second. It was as if God stuck out His hand between me and the other car. It did not hit me. I recognized immediately that it was the protection of God even though I was a sinner. His angels intervened once again. Thank God for mercy, grace, and favor.

God's hands were on my life after I had surgery in the mid-1980s. Actually, His hands were on me before, during, and after surgery. I had removal of fibroids vaginally. On three occasions, I had hemorrhaged. The first time was when I had jumped awaken out of a dream. I discovered I was bleeding/hemorrhaging. I went back to the doctor who had performed my surgery. He packed me vaginally with gauzes. I went home. A few days later, the same thing happened. I was sweeping the floor. I started hemorrhaging. I went back to the same doctor. Again, he packed me vaginally with gauzes. He asked me if I was having sex. I said, "No!" I was not crazy enough to have sex after surgery. I went home.

A few days later, I was using the bathroom. While sitting on the commode, I was hemorrhaging badly. Russell and I were dating at that time. He was at work. I called my cousin who was home from the Army. He came to pick me up. I told him to take me straight to Duke University Hospital. I was not going back to the doctor that had been packing me with gauzes. On the way, my cousin had to stop for gas. While he was pumping the gas, I felt the blood just gushing from me onto his car seat. I felt really bad for messing up his seat, but I could not control the bleeding. When we arrived at Duke Hospital, he had to carry me inside. No sooner than we walked through the doors of Duke Hospital, one of the nurses asked, "Who got shot?" That's how bad I was bleeding.

The doctors discussed with me that depended on what they saw that I may have to have a hysterectomy. I told the doctors, "Just go ahead and give me a hysterectomy anyway." They informed me that they could not just give me a hysterectomy, and that I would have to have a reason to have it. The doctors took me into the operating room. They did their thing. When I woke up from the procedure, they told me that they did not give me a hysterectomy. The doctor said that all I needed was "one stitch." After all those hemorrhaging episodes, I needed one little stitch. To think that I could have died over needing one stitch. Praise God that was all I needed.

I recovered fully. Thank God that I was fully covered by His blood. I was not saved then, but God's hand was still on my life. Had He removed His hand, I would have died in my sins. That is why I love Him like I do. That is why I praise Him like I do.

In 1999, I ended up having a hysterectomy anyway. I had fibroid tumors. I was constantly in pain to the degree of birth pangs at times. Prior to my hysterectomy, I heard testimonies of women who had the surgery. Most of them had good outcomes. I said to God, "God, I've heard the testimonies of others, but I want You to do something for me. I want my own testimony." I had a C-section when my son was born in 1987; therefore, the doctor wanted to cut along the same lines to prevent further scarring. After surgery, he told me that my tumor was so big that it had protruded through my uterus. Therefore, they had to remove my uterus. I had a successful surgery, believe it or not, without any pain associated with it whatsoever. That's what God did for me. I was pain-free. Nobody but God could have bestowed His mercy, grace, and favor upon me. I asked, and I received. I tried Him. He proved Himself to me once again.

I would usually get bored with a job after about four years. In 2005, I received my RN license. In 2010, I decided to venture out from where I was working to another job on the other side of the town. After being at the new job for a few months,

I realized that I had made a big mistake. I called the Director of Nursing at my former job to let her know that I wanted to come back. Trust me, I was not too proud to ask. She said, "Yes." I was super happy. There was a job opening where I knew several people whom I had encountered in the past. I wanted that job. I made a radical move. I claimed that job. I rode around on the parking lot three times: one for the Father, one for the Son, and one for the Holy Ghost. I would have ridden around it seven times representing the fall of the Jericho wall, but someone came out of the building. I felt sure that if that person saw me continue to circle the parking lot that law enforcement would have been called.

I received a call for an interview. Shortly afterward, the supervisor told me that I had the job, but it was not official yet. I waited and waited for the offer. Two months had passed. I knew in my heart of hearts that the job was mine. I knew it in my spirit. I called the supervisor to see what was taking so long. She informed me that she wanted to hire me, but the higher ups wanted someone else in the position. She was disappointed. So was I. But my faith in God granting me the position did not wane because I still knew that the job was mine.

Shortly afterward, I received a call for a different position. I knew God was working. I told God that wherever He wanted me to go, that is where I will go. I was content with God's plan. I accepted the other position. In the process of making arrangements to go into the alternative position, I received a phone call. I was offered the original position that I had claimed when I rode around the parking lot three times. God did not disappoint. Won't He do it! Favor ain't fair y'all. If the mercies and favors of God were in color, I would be surrounded by continuous rainbows.

Let me share one of God's favors that still make me in awe of who He is. I mentioned in an earlier paragraph that I had purchased a home while my husband and I were on break from our marriage. Prior to purchasing that home, I had searched diligently for a place of my own. I knew I did not want to live in the city. I did not want to live deep in the country either. I remembered being very frustrated because I could not find anything that I desired. I said to God, *God, I don't feel like you heard me.*

Right after that, the Holy Spirit said to me to turn right on this particular road. I said, *Lord, I have been on that road, and I haven't seen a house, but I will be obedient anyway.* I turned on this road. Lo and behold, there was a sign in the yard that said FOR SALE. I was like, what? The driveway went around to the back so I could not see if anyone was home. I decided to drive around the back of the home. As soon as I drove to the back of the home, there were two cars. One was the realtor, and the other one was a client interested in the home. They had just finished their business, and the client was preparing to leave.

The realtor asked me if I wanted to see the home. Of course, I said, "Yes." When I entered the home, I fell in love with it. It had everything that I had desired: front porch, back deck, double fireplace, even down to the hydrangea bush. The realtor told me he had just put that sign up that same day. I knew this was God's doing, God's favor. After seeing the home, I told the realtor that I probably would contact him the next day to place an offer. Later that night, I contacted the realtor to make an offer on that home. I knew beyond the shadow of a doubt that God had ordained that home for me. I was not about to let it get away from me. You cannot tell me that was not my God. I am so grateful to have heard in my spirit the Holy Spirit speak to me. I am grateful for being a doer and not just a hearer. He said in His Word that we have not because we ask not. Believe me, I don't mind asking my Papa God for whatever I need or want. If only you knew of the things I have received just for asking.

And whatever things you ask in prayer, believing, you will receive. (Matthew 21:22 NKJV)

Let me share the ironic thing about this home. This home was just a street over from where I had lived with my husband. We were neighbors. I knew God was up to something, but I didn't dare guess what God was up to.

> For My thoughts are not your thoughts, nor are your ways My ways, saith the Lord. (Isaiah 55:8 NKJV)

God apparently knew that my husband and I had unfinished business. Needless to say, I stayed in that new home for two years before my husband and I had reconciled. Let's just say we were more than neighbors for the last one and a half years before reconciling. It was all good. We were still married. I cannot share too much as this may be book number two. My husband says, "Not!"

Prior to purchasing this home, I was supposed to put a down payment on another home about ten miles out of the city limits. It was a brick home. I did not hear the Holy Spirit's voice regarding the brick home. However, one night in particular, I was supposed to sign a contract for the brick home and put down my deposit. I went back to that home just to lay eyes on it again before signing the contract. When I went back that night, the highway sign was missing. I became paranoid and thought that vandalism had occurred in the neighborhood. Therefore, I backed out of the deal and did not sign the contract. It was in God's plan. That was not the home ordained for me.

When I think about it now and the distance of the brick home, I believe that if I had chosen that brick home out of the city limits that my husband and I would not have had that close tie to reconnect, rekindle, and reconcile. One of my favorite scriptures is Matthew 21:22. That is the scripture that I stood on believing God to restore my marriage. I had written this on a vision board in 2016. We reconciled in 2017. God is good all the time, and all the time God is good.

Speaking of asking, believing, and receiving, I have to share this. Remember I told you about being dismissed from working at this clinic and that this clinic had great perks? Each year we had an annual inspection of narcotics from the DEA. This particular year, we aced the inspection. The doctor who owned the clinic wanted to reward us for a great job that we had done. We all had to decide collectively of a group reward. One wanted to go fishing. One wanted to go on a picnic. One wanted to go bowling. Well, I said I wanted to go to a nice restaurant, and I wanted to be waited on at the table. I also said that I wanted a two-hundred-fifty-dollar bonus. But then I thought about all the clinics that this doctor owned, I changed the amount to a five-hundred-dollar bonus.

One of the rewards that we had received was that we all went out to eat at a steak house. I thought maybe the bonus would be presented at dinner, but nothing else was said about another reward. I said to myself, *I know this is not all the reward we are getting!* We went back to work with no mention of another reward. However, when we received our paychecks, guess what? Our five-hundred-dollar bonus was in our checks. Whoop, whoop! When one of my coworkers saw her check, she came to me and said, "Darlene, you did it. We got our five-hundred-dollar bonus."

I said, "No, God did it. We have because we asked." I would not dare take the credit because all the glory belongs to God.

On one job that I had, my boss was a rewarder of degrees. He favored degrees. In my position as an RN, he continued to say that when you have a degree, you can ask for anything. After him saying it so many times, I decided to put him to the test. At that time, I was getting an hourly wage. I no longer wanted an hourly wage. I made a bold move and asked for a salary. This scene is like something that you see in the movies. The boss asked me what the salary amount that I was requesting. I jotted down the amount on a piece of paper and slid it across his desk to him. He looked at it. I left his office after that. He neither said he agreed or disagreed. When the paychecks rolled around, guess what? I received my adjusted salary rate. When we seek God's kingdom and His righteousness then all these things (favor) will be added unto us. I guess you can say that I have history with God.

May God's favor be upon you and a thousand generations, and your family and your children and their children and their children. God is for you. Amen. (Elevation Worship—The Blessing)

CONCLUSION

Okay, now you know most of my imperfections. But in God's eyes, I am perfect. I am a beautiful mess. My bishop preached one Sunday about a Beautiful Mess. I said under my breath at my seat, *Yep, that's me.* What the enemy has meant for evil, God has turned it around for my good.

I am not ashamed to speak my truth. My life is like an open book. It is like I told my husband when we first met, "What you see is what you get. I am no more or no less." As you can see, I am very transparent. I share my testimonies/truths to say that if you have been or are going through some of the things that I have experienced or other experiences, that God will bring you through. He has no respect of persons. What He did for me, He can do for you.

> But you must learn to endure everything, so you will be completely mature and not lacking in anything. (James 1:4 CEV)

Cast all your worries and cares
to God, for He cares about you. (1
Peter 5:7)

Take Him at his Word. When I look at my life and all the hell that I had experienced, I take another look and see the joy of the Lord. I see the righteous right hand of the Lord upholding me. I did not understand then why I went through the things that I did go through. I know now that sometimes when we go through things, that it is not about us. It is to help the next person along their journey by sharing our testimonies.

Also, it's about growing my faith. Even though it did not feel good when I went through, it was most definitely working for my good. Everything that I had went through drew me closer to the Lord. My testimony, my trials, my failures have drawn me closer to God. As my bishop says, God "dragged me" back to Him. I am determined to serve God with my whole heart, especially knowing that He had never left me or forsaken me in my mess. "If I ascend to heaven, You are there; If I make my bed in hell, behold You are there" (Psalm 139:8 NKJV).

I am reminded of the Footprints poem, especially the Lord's reply:

> My son (daughter), my precious
> child
> I love you and I would never leave
> you
> During your times of trial and
> suffering,
> When you saw only one set of
> footprints,
> It was then that I carried you.

Though I did not know it then as a child, I know now that God was always there carrying me when I felt I could not go any farther. One of the scriptures that helped me survive my trials in my youth was that God said in His Word that He would not put more on me than I could bear.

> No temptation has overtaken
> you except such as is common
> to man; but God is faithful, who
> will not allow you to be tempted
> beyond what you are able, but with
> the temptation will also make the
> way of escape, that you may be able
> to bear it. (1 Corinthians 10:13
> NKJV)

Therefore, I knew that if it was on me, that I could get through it. I did not think that I would overcome the pain, guilt or the shame, but God has delivered me. Jesus overcame the world; therefore, I can overcome life's fiery trials. I am free. Praise the Lord. No more chains holding me.

The Serenity Prayer is one of my favorite prayers that helped me in my life.

> God grant me the serenity to accept the things I cannot change, Courage to change the things I can, and the wisdom to know the difference.

I used to take on people's burdens, their pains. I was a people pleaser. I was their problem solver, their peace maker. I was their bank account. I was whatever they needed me to be. But then I realized that I could no longer carry other people's weight. I had to get some of their weight off of me. It was dragging me down.

Bishop preached one Sunday about, "If it is not on your plate, then don't mess with it." That was one of my problems. I was putting other people's stuff on my plate. My plate was spilling over, and I was trying to clean up everyone's mess whether they asked me or not. I knew that I could not fix everybody's problems, though I tried. I really tried. It was impossible for me to do it. I had to pray. I had to learn the difference between what I could and what I could not do. I had to weigh the consequences of accepting things I could not change. I had to find the strength and the courage. It was extremely hard to find my voice. But I did. One "No" at a time. Wisdom stepped in. I was able to distinguish the difference. I was able to breathe.

Now one of the things that I tell people who are going through is to "just breathe." On an airplane, the stewardess used to instruct in an emergency that you put on your oxygen mask first. It would be hard for me to do that, especially if someone sitting next to me needs it just as much as I do. I am not sure if I would totally give it up. I believe I would alternate using the oxygen mask so we both could have a chance at surviving. I cannot save the world, but I can do my part. I may not have it altogether. I don't have to. All I need to do is trust the process and trust my God in my process.

Many years ago, there was this woman who was crying her eyes out and leaning against the wall at the hospital. She apparently had received some bad news. I wanted to go over and hug her, but I did not. I was with my family, and we were on our way out of the hospital. To this day, I regret not hugging her because I know what it feels like to be in so much pain with no one to ease the burden. I said after that day that I will never walk past anyone who is hurting. I will take the time to stop and speak encouraging words in their lives or lend my shoulder to cry upon.

We walk pass people every day not knowing what they are dealing with, not knowing their genesis. After that incident, I try to be intentional to spread joy into people's lives. I want them to feel better when leaving my presence than before entering into my presence. What we say can either make or break them. My husband says sometimes that my kindness may get me in trouble. I tell him that people may mistake my kindness as a weakness, but I assured him that they find out real soon that my kindness is not a weakness. I promise. My intention is to let people, especially my sister queens, know that someone cares about what they are going through and they do not have to walk their journey alone.

Now that I have shared my genesis (trials/tribulations) and my exodus (deliverance/restoration), I trust that you do not judge me but rejoice with me for the marvelous things that God has done in my life and is doing for me, a sinner saved by grace through faith. I thank God, that I do not look like what I have been through simply because it was a beautiful exchange. Jesus died so that I can live. Only the love of God could break the chains that held me in bondage. I thank God for being my Redeemer, my Healer, my Restorer, my Stronghold, my Sustainer of Life.

Now my life is full and purposeful. I purposely now keep a smile on my face because of genuine love and joy in my heart. I choose to have a joyful spirit because of His Spirit in me. My purpose is to speak life into others' lives. I know that my calling is to minister to the hearts of women especially, but also to those who are hurting. So beloved, whatever is ailing you, I pray that you receive your healing, your deliverance, your breakthrough. I pray that you find the courage to find your voice. I pray that you know it is okay to say you are not okay. I pray that you do not suffer in silence. I pray that you speak your truth. I pray that you esteem one another. I pray that you lean on each other. I pray that self-care is a priority. I pray that you know you have an exodus; you will come out of bondage. I pray that your purpose is revealed and that you walk in it courageously. I pray for you continuously.

Precious, you cannot do it alone. You need the Spirit of God in your heart. He is your Savior. He sees you (El Roi). He knows you by name. He knows what you are going through. He is with you in the midst of your storm. He created you for His purposes. Receive Him today so that you can have a Holy Ghost life-changing experience. Romans 10:9 tells us to confess with your mouth and believe in your heart that God has raised Jesus from the dead, you shall be saved. God is waiting with His arms outstretched for you to enter into His presence. He is waiting to receive you. He is waiting for you to dwell in His secret place. Run. Do not walk. Time is of the essence.

I thank God for stirring up gifts inside of me. A gift is to be shared, not withheld. Just as He has given His free gift of the Holy Spirit to me, I share my gift with you. I pray that my book has encouraged you to walk in your truth. When we walk in our truth, that is when the healing process begins and we can truly love ourselves first and then others. Beloved, one last thing I leave with you are Roses to remind you how beautiful, multifaceted, and loved you really are.

ROSES

Beloved, you are like roses. You are beautiful. You are delicate. You are elegant. You are tender. You are a sweet-smelling aroma. You are desired. You stand out. The stem of thorns represents your pain, circumstances, trauma, secrets. The thorns are temporal. God is the florist. He prunes you. He removes the thorns and dead branches that plague you. He kisses your wound and heals that area that was pricked. That is for eternity. Unfold your petals and blossom. You are bountiful. You are resilient. You are loved. You are chosen. Do what you were designed to do: draw others to you to behold your beauty.

Darlene W. Parrish

ABOUT THE AUTHOR

Darlene Wilkerson Parrish is a wife, mother, grandmother, and author. She has been married to Russell for thirty-one years. She and her husband have two children (Russell Jr. and Chantel) and nine grandchildren (Josiah, Aaliyah, Tristin, TyJuan, Shiyonna, Camiya, Alivia, Mira, and Amin). A host of these grandchildren adopted Darlene and Russell as their grandparents, which they are truly honored.

Darlene has an Associate's Degree in Medical Office Technology. She also has an Associate's Degree in Nursing (RN). She has since retired from full-time employment. She is currently a student in Northeastern Regional Bible College, where she is pursuing a Bachelor's Degree in Christian Counseling. She believes her calling is to minister to the hearts of the broken, bruised, and battered women.

Darlene is super passionate about advocating for those who are in need and those who do not have a voice. She is a natural encourager and believes in speaking "life" into others. She has started a support group in the community called JUST BREATHE Women's Support Group. The purpose is to create a sisterhood of support to let women know that they do not have to walk alone on their journey. She is an active member at Cornerstone Christian Community Church. She is also active in her community. One of her favorite organizations that she volunteers is with Meals on Wheels. One of her favorite sayings is, "Life is like a coin. You only get to spend it once. Don't get shortchanged."

CPSIA information can be obtained
at www.ICGtesting.com
Printed in the USA
BVHW081510230822
645283BV00005B/297

9 781685 264802